HBR'S 10 MUST READS

The definitive
management ideas
of the year from
Harvard Business Review.

2022

HBR's 10 Must Reads series is the definitive collection of ideas and best practices for aspiring and experienced leaders alike. These books offer essential reading selected from the pages of *Harvard Business Review* on topics critical to the success of every manager.

Titles include:

The definitive
management ideas
of the year from
Harvard Business Review.

HARVARD BUSINESS REVIEW PRESS
Boston, Massachusetts

Library of Congress Cataloging-in-Publication Data

Names: Harvard Business Review Press, issuing body.
Title: HBR's 10 must reads 2022: the definitive management ideas of the year from Harvard Business Review.
Other titles: HBR's 10 must reads (2022) | Harvard Business Review's 10 must reads | HBR's 10 must reads (Series)
Description: Boston, MA : Harvard Business Review Press, [2021] | Series: HBR's 10 must reads series | Includes index.
Identifiers: LCCN 2021022666 (print) | LCCN 2021022667 (ebook) | ISBN 9781647822132 (paperback) | ISBN 9781647822149 (ebook)
Subjects: LCSH: Management.
Classification: LCC HD31.2 .H369 2021 (print) | LCC HD31.2 (ebook) | DDC 658—dc23
LC record available at https://lccn.loc.gov/2021022666
LC ebook record available at https://lccn.loc.gov/2021022667

ISBN: 978-1-64782-213-2
eISBN: 978-1-64782-214-9

The paper used in this publication meets the requirements of the American National Standard for Permanence of Paper for Publications and Documents in Libraries and Archives Z39.48-1992.

Contents

As our editorial team read through the past year's issues of *Harvard Business Review* to select the articles for this volume, a feeling of hope emerged among us. After many trying months of social distancing, adjusting to remote work, political unrest, a worldwide recession, and illuminating social justice movements, vaccine rollouts were ramping up globally, and a brighter future felt within reach. When we chose these pieces, we tried not only to look back at the year that was but also to imagine what leaders would need at the dawn of 2022 to thrive in the new normal.

More often than ever before, articles HBR published were a direct response to current events. We covered the issue of anxiety and work for the first time because the alarming increase of people experiencing anxiety became impossible for leaders to ignore. The crises pushed many people to rethink their careers, what they expect from their employers, and how they'd like to work—making it a prime time for brushing up on job negotiation skills. These articles reminded us that life would keep going on in spite of the chaos. We saw that in explorations of compassionate leadership, the best ways to grow an innovative culture, and the continuing rise of machine learning. Other pieces looked at trends already underway that had accelerated over the past year. Some organizations were working remotely before 2020, but the pandemic created a need to swiftly get up to speed with the right technology and the best team practices for working from anywhere. And although inequality and bias have been unresolved workplace issues for centuries, recent events have forced us to reexamine what it means to have a truly inclusive, diverse workplace—and to reflect on what hasn't worked in the past.

The challenges of 2020 revealed where we should start making changes for a better year ahead. The old ways aren't coming back, and in many cases we wouldn't want them to. As you read through this collection, we hope these articles inspire hope and help you feel prepared for what's next.

We start off with **"Begin with Trust,"** because as Frances Frei and Anne Morriss say, "Trust is the basis for almost everything we do." It's the reason we're willing to exchange our hard-earned paychecks for goods and services, to pledge our lives to another person in marriage, and to cast a ballot for someone who will represent our interests. Trust is also essential for leaders who strive to empower other people as a result of their presence and to ensure that the impact of their leadership continues beyond their tenure. The more trust you build, the easier it is to practice that kind of leadership. How can leaders start? By being authentic, exercising sound judgment, and showing empathy. Frei and Morriss explain how to assess your strengths and weaknesses when it comes to trust and offer advice for building the three components of trust.

In **"Cultural Innovation,"** Douglas Holt argues that companies struggle with innovation because they put all their chips on one innovation paradigm—what he calls *better mousetraps*. Fortunately, there is a better way to innovate. In consumer markets, innovation often proceeds according to a logic Holt calls *cultural innovation*. With better-mousetraps innovation, companies focus on outdoing competitors on existing notions of value. With cultural innovation, you change the understanding of "valuable." Using the stories of the Ford Explorer's reinvention of the family car and how Blue Buffalo turned the culture of dog food on its head, Holt reveals the strategic principles that allow companies to pursue cultural innovation.

"Co-opetition"—cooperating with a competitor to achieve a common goal or get ahead—has been gaining traction for three decades. Yet many companies are still uncomfortable with the concept and miss the promising opportunities it presents. In **"The Rules of Co-opetition,"** Adam Brandenburger and Barry Nalebuff offer a framework for deciding whether to team up with a rival and how to manage the relationship, drawing on examples from DHL, UPS, Google, and Yahoo. Co-opetition requires teams to think both competitively and cooperatively—at the same time. Firms that learn to do so can gain an important edge.

Cooperation is also key to successful negotiation. In **"Negotiating Your Next Job,"** Hannah Riley Bowles and Bobbi Thomason encourage readers seeking to advance their careers to think strategically about not just what they want but how to get it. The authors draw on their work coaching executives and their cross-cultural research to propose four steps that can prepare you to negotiate: Think broadly about your long-term career goals, be mindful of what type of opportunity you're asking for, arm yourself with the necessary information, and connect with people who can be helpful in making your case. Be specific and realistic, they argue, and you're more likely to achieve success.

Although many workers dealt with anxiety before 2020, for some the uncertainty and stress of the pandemic brought it on for the first time. In **"Leading Through Anxiety,"** Morra Aarons-Mele starts a productive, much-needed conversation about anxiety in the workplace and how we can reframe its negative reputation. She explains that although anxiety is uncomfortable, it isn't always counterproductive. Because managing anxiety can make us more comfortable with uncomfortable feelings, it can prompt us to react quickly to threats. And when channeled thoughtfully, it can make us better leaders in a crisis. But unchecked, it zaps energy and clouds decisions. In this article Aarons-Mele offers advice on how to inspire and encourage your team even when you're struggling yourself.

Products and services that rely on machine learning don't always lead to ethical or accurate choices. Sometimes they cause investment losses, for instance, or biased hiring, or car accidents. And as machine-learning-based AI offerings proliferate across markets, the companies creating them face major new risks. Executives need to understand and mitigate the technology's potential downside. In **"When Machine Learning Goes Off the Rails,"** Boris Babic, I. Glenn Cohen, Theodoros Evgeniou, and Sara Gerke provide a guide to managing the risks.

Twenty-five years ago Robin J. Ely and David A. Thomas made the groundbreaking argument that to fully benefit from increased racial and gender diversity, organizations must adopt a learning orientation and be willing to change the corporate culture and power structure. In the time since, organizations have largely failed to do so and are no closer to reaping diversity's benefits. Instead, business leaders misconstrue or ignore what abundant research has made clear: Increasing the numbers of traditionally underrepresented people in your workforce does not automatically produce good results. Now, in **"Getting Serious About Diversity,"** the authors reevaluate and update their argument and highlight the key actions for leaders looking to make real change.

As intractable as it may seem, racism in the workplace can be effectively addressed with the right information, incentives, and investment. Robert Livingston argues that because organizations are small, autonomous entities that afford leaders a high level of control over norms and policies, they are ideal sites for doing so. In **"How to Promote Racial Equity in the Workplace,"** Livingston walks readers through the five stages of a process for making profound and sustainable progress toward this goal in your organization.

The pandemic has hastened a rise in remote working for knowledge-based organizations. This has notable benefits: Companies can save on real estate costs, hire and utilize talent globally, mitigate immigration issues, and experience productivity gains, while workers can enjoy geographic flexibility. At the same time, concerns include how to communicate across time zones, share knowledge that isn't yet codified, socialize virtually and prevent professional isolation, protect client data, and avoid slacking. In **"Our Work-from-Anywhere Future,"** Prithwiraj (Raj) Choudhury highlights best practices that can help leaders decide whether remote working is right for their organizations.

"A More Sustainable Supply Chain" tackles the disconnect between the commitment of multinational corporations (MNCs) to sustainability and the reality of their suppliers. MNCs are pledging to procure the materials and services they need from companies committed to fair labor practices and environmental protections. But their suppliers—and their suppliers' suppliers—often violate sustainability standards, exposing MNCs to serious financial and social risks. To explore this problem—and identify solutions—Verónica H. Villena and Dennis A. Gioia studied the supply networks of three MNCs deemed to be sustainability leaders.

To close this collection, we take a fascinating look at a widely admired company whose internal workings have often been unknowable to outsiders. In **"How Apple Is Organized for Innovation,"** Joel M. Podolny and Morten T. Hansen discuss the innovation benefits and leadership challenges of Apple's distinctive and ever-evolving organizational model in the belief that it may be useful for other companies competing in rapidly changing environments. When Steve Jobs returned to Apple, in 1997, it had a conventional structure for a company of its size and scope. It was divided into business units, each with its own P&L responsibilities. Believing that conventional management had stifled innovation, Jobs laid off the general managers of all the business units (in a single day), put the entire company under one P&L, and combined the disparate functional departments of the business units into one functional organization. Although such a structure is common for small entrepreneurial firms, Apple—remarkably—retains it today, even though the company is nearly 40 times as large in terms of revenue and far more complex than it was in 1997.

Keeping up with business trends and synthesizing the best ideas is important—and time-consuming—work for today's leaders. With this volume, we've done the heavy lifting for you. Despite the challenges of the past year, you can learn much from these articles as you lead your business forward. We hope they prepare you for a better year ahead and set you on the right track for a prosperous future.

—The Editors

The definitive
management ideas
of the year from
Harvard Business Review.

2022

Begin with Trust

by Frances Frei and Anne Morriss

ON A SPRING AFTERNOON IN 2017, Travis Kalanick, then the CEO of Uber, walked into a conference room at the company's Bay Area headquarters. One of us, Frances, was waiting for him. Meghan Joyce, the company's general manager for the United States and Canada, had reached out to us, hoping that we could guide the company as it sought to heal from a series of deep, self-inflicted wounds. We had a track record of helping organizations, many of them founder-led, tackle messy leadership and culture challenges.

We were skeptical about Uber. Everything we'd read about the company suggested it had little hope of redemption. At the time, the company was an astonishingly disruptive and successful start-up, but its success seemed to have come at the price of basic decency. In early 2017, for example, when taxi drivers went on strike in New York City to protest President Trump's travel ban, Uber appeared to have used tactics to profit from the situation—a move that prompted widespread outrage and a #deleteUber campaign. A month later, not long before the meeting, an Uber engineer named Susan Fowler had blogged courageously about her experiences of harassment and discrimination at the company, which caused more outrage. Footage of Kalanick had then emerged, in a video that went viral, of his interaction with an Uber driver, where he appeared dismissive of the pain of earning a living in a post-Uber world. Additional charges leveled at the company in this period reinforced Uber's reputation as a cold-blooded operator that would do almost anything to win.

Despite our skepticism, Frances had gone to California to hear Kalanick out. (Anne was building her own company at the time, so

1

she took a back seat on the project.) As Frances waited for him to make his entrance, she braced herself for the smug CEO she'd read about. But that wasn't who walked in. Kalanick arrived humbled and introspective. He had thought a lot about how the cultural values he'd instilled in the company—the very values that had fueled Uber's success—had also been misused and distorted on his watch. He expressed deep respect for what his team had achieved but also acknowledged that he'd put some people in leadership roles without giving them the training or mentorship to be effective. Whatever mistakes Kalanick had made up to that point, he revealed a sincere desire to do the right thing as a leader.

We regrouped back in Cambridge, Massachusetts, and debated whether to take on the project. There were lots of reasons to stay far away from it. The work would be hard and its outcome uncertain, to say nothing of the brutal commute. Uber's workforce was frustrated, and the brand was becoming toxic. But we realized that if we could help get Uber back on the right path, then we could offer a road map to countless others trying to restore humanity to organizations that had lost their way. So we signed on.

After making that decision, we knew exactly where to start. With trust.

Empowerment Leadership

We think of trust as precious, and yet it's the basis for almost everything we do as civilized people. Trust is the reason we're willing to exchange our hard-earned paychecks for goods and services, pledge our lives to another person in marriage, cast a ballot for someone who will represent our interests. We rely on laws and contracts as safety nets, but even they are ultimately built on trust in the institutions that enforce them. We don't know that justice will be served if something goes wrong, but we have enough faith in the system that we're willing to make high-stakes deals with relative strangers.

Trust is also one of the most essential forms of capital a leader has. Building trust, however, often requires thinking about leadership from a new perspective. The traditional leadership narrative

Idea in Brief

The Starting Point

The traditional leadership narrative is all about you: your talents, charisma, and moments of courage and instinct. But real leadership is about your people and creating the conditions for them to fully realize their own capacity and power. To do this, you have to develop stores of trust.

The Challenge

How do leaders build trust? By focusing on its core drivers: authenticity, logic, and empathy.

People tend to trust you when they think they're interacting with the real you, when they have faith in your judgment and competence, and when they believe you care about them.

The Way Forward

When leaders have trouble with trust, it's usually because they're weak on one of those three drivers. To develop or restore trust, identify which driver you're "wobbly" on, and then work on strengthening it.

is all about you: your vision and strategy; your ability to make the tough calls and rally the troops; your talents, your charisma, your heroic moments of courage and instinct. But leadership really isn't about you. It's about empowering other people as a result of your presence, and about making sure that the impact of your leadership continues into your absence.

That's the fundamental principle we've learned in the course of dedicating our careers to making leaders and organizations better. Your job as a leader is to create the conditions for your people to fully realize their own capacity and power. And that's true not only when you're in the trenches with them but also when you're not around and even—this is the cleanest test—when you've permanently moved on from the team. We call it empowerment leadership. The more trust you build, the more possible it is to practice this kind of leadership.

The Core Drivers of Trust

So how do you build up stores of this foundational leadership capital? In our experience, trust has three core drivers: authenticity, logic, and empathy. People tend to trust you when they believe they are interacting with the real you (authenticity), when they have faith in your judgment and competence (logic), and when they feel that you care about them (empathy). When trust is lost, it can almost always be traced back to a breakdown in one of these three drivers.

People don't always realize how the information (or more often, the misinformation) that they're broadcasting may undermine their own trustworthiness. What's worse, stress tends to amplify the problem, causing people to double down on behaviors that make others skeptical. For example, they might unconsciously mask their true selves in a job interview, even though that's precisely the type of less-than-fully-authentic behavior that reduces their chance of being hired.

The good news is that most of us generate a stable pattern of trust signals, which means a small change in behavior can go a long way. In moments when trust is broken, or fails to get any real traction, it's usually the same driver that has gone wobbly on us—authenticity, empathy, or logic. We call this driver your "trust wobble." In simple terms, it's the driver that's most likely to fail you.

Everybody, it turns out, has a trust wobble. To build trust as a leader, you first need to figure out what yours is.

Build It, and They Will Come

To identify your wobble, think of a recent moment when you were not trusted as much as you wanted to be. Maybe you lost an important sale or didn't get a stretch assignment. Maybe someone simply doubted your ability to execute. With that moment in mind, do something hard: Give the other person in your story the benefit of the doubt. Let's call that person your "skeptic." Assume that your skeptic's reservations were valid and that you were the one responsible for the breakdown in trust. This exercise only works if you own it.

If you had to choose from our three trust drivers, which would you say went wobbly on you in this situation? Did your skeptic feel you were misrepresenting some part of yourself or your story? If so, that's an authenticity problem. Did your skeptic feel you might be

The trust triangle

Trust has three drivers: authenticity, logic, and empathy. When trust is lost, it can almost always be traced back to a breakdown in one of them. To build trust as a leader, you first need to figure out which driver you "wobble" on.

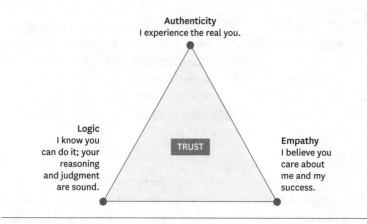

putting your own interests first? If so, that's an empathy problem. Did your skeptic question the rigor of your analysis or your ability to execute on an ambitious plan? If so, that's a logic problem.

Now stand back and try to look at your pattern of wobbles across multiple incidents. Pick three or four interactions that stand out to you, for whatever reason, and do a quick trust diagnostic for each one. What does your typical wobble seem to be? Does the pattern change under stress or with different kinds of stakeholders? For example, do you wobble on one trait with your direct reports but on a different one with people who have authority over you? That's not uncommon.

This exercise works best if you bring at least one person along for your diagnostic ride, ideally someone who knows you well. Sharing your analysis can be clarifying—even liberating—and will help you test and refine your hypothesis. In our experience, about 20% of self-assessments need a round of revision, so choose a partner who can keep you honest. Consider going back and testing your analysis directly by speaking openly about it with your skeptic. This conversation alone can be a powerful way to rebuild trust. When you take responsibility for a wobble, you reveal your humanity (authenticity) and analytic chops (logic) while communicating your commitment to the relationship (empathy).

Overcoming Your Wobble

Over the past decade we've helped all kinds of leaders—from seasoned politicians to Millennial entrepreneurs to the heads of multibillion-dollar companies—wrestle with trust issues. In doing so, we've learned a lot about strategies you can deploy to overcome your own trust wobbles. Let's explore what's most effective for each of the drivers in our trust triangle.

Empathy

Most high-achieving leaders struggle with this one. Signaling a lack of empathy is a major barrier to empowerment leadership. If people think you care more about yourself than about others, they won't trust you enough to lead them.

Empathy wobbles are common among people who are analytical and driven to learn. They often get impatient with those who aren't similarly motivated or who take longer than they do to understand something. Additionally, the tools and experience of the modern workplace continually distract or prevent us from demonstrating empathy, by imposing 24-hour demands on our time and putting at our disposal all sorts of technologies that compete for our attention at any given moment. Our beeping and buzzing devices constantly assert our self-importance, sometimes smack in the middle of interactions with the very people we're working to empower and lead.

We advise empathy wobblers to pay close attention to their behavior in group settings, particularly when other people have the floor. Consider what often happens in a meeting: When it kicks off, most people feel very engaged. But as soon as empathy wobblers understand the concepts under discussion and have contributed their ideas, they lose interest. Their engagement plummets and remains low until the gathering (mercifully) comes to an end. Instead of paying attention, they often multitask, check their phones, engage in flamboyant displays of boredom—anything to make clear that this meeting is beneath them. Unfortunately, the cost of these indulgences is trust. If you signal that you matter more than everyone else, why should anyone trust the direction you're going in? What's in it for the rest of us to come along?

There's a basic solution to this problem. Instead of focusing on what you need in that meeting, work to ensure that everyone else gets what they need. Take radical responsibility for the others in the room. Share the burden of moving the dialogue forward, even if it's not your meeting. Search for the resonant examples that will bring the concepts to life, and don't disengage until everyone else in the room understands. This is almost impossible to do if texting or checking email is an option, so put away your devices. Everyone knows you're not taking notes on their good ideas.

Indeed, the last thing we'll say on empathy is this: If you do nothing else to change your behavior, put away your phone more frequently. Put it truly away, out of sight and out of reach, not just flipped over for a few minutes at a time. You'll be amazed at the change in the quality of your interactions and your ability to build trust.

Logic

If people don't always have confidence in the rigor of your ideas, or if they don't have full faith in your ability to deliver on them, then logic is probably your wobble. If they don't trust your judgment, why would they want you at the wheel?

When logic is the problem, we advise going back to the data. Root the case you're making in sound evidence, speak about the things you know to be true beyond a reasonable doubt, and then—this is the hard part—stop there. One reason Larry Bird was such an extraordinary basketball player was that he only took shots he knew he could reliably make. That choice made him different from other great players who let ego and adrenaline cloud their shooting judgment. Bird studied and practiced so relentlessly that by the time the ball left his hands in the heat of competition, he knew exactly where it was going. If logic is your wobble, take Bird's example and learn to "play within yourself."

Once you get comfortable with how that feels, start expanding what you know. Along the way, make an effort to learn from other people. Their insight is among your most valuable resources, but to access it, you must be willing to reveal that you don't have all the answers—something leaders often resist. Engaging people about their experience has the additional benefit of communicating who you are and what energizes you professionally—an authenticity boost.

For most logic wobblers, however, rigor isn't the issue. Much of the time, the problem is the perception of wobbly logic rather than the reality of it. Why does this happen? Because they're not communicating their ideas effectively.

There are generally two ways to communicate complex thoughts. The first takes your audience on a journey, with twists and turns and context and dramatic tension, until they eventually get to the payoff. Many of the world's best storytellers use this technique. You can visualize this approach by imagining an inverted triangle. The journeying storyteller starts at the top, at the inverted base of the triangle, and traces an enchantingly meandering route down to its point.

If logic is your wobble, however, that's a risky path to take. With all that circuitous journeying, you're likely to lose your audience along the way rather than build trust in your judgment. Listeners may even abandon you at one of your narrative turns.

To avoid that, try flipping the imaginary triangle upright. Start with your main point, or headline, at the top of the triangle, and then work your way down, building a base of reinforcing evidence. This approach signals a clarity of vision and a full command of the facts. Everyone has a much better chance of following your logic. Even if you get interrupted along the way, you'll at least have had a chance to communicate your key idea.

Authenticity

If people feel they're not getting access to the "real" you—to a full and complete accounting of what you know, think, and feel—then you probably have an authenticity wobble.

A quick test: How different is your professional persona from the one that shows up around family and friends? If there's a sharp difference, what are you getting in return for masking or minimizing certain parts of yourself? What's the payoff?

Being your "real self" sounds nice in theory, but there can be powerful reasons for holding back certain truths. The calculation can be highly practical at times, if wrenching—as in deciding to stay closeted in a workplace that's hostile to queer identities. There may also be times when expressing your authentic feelings may risk harmful consequences: Women, for example, are disproportionately penalized for displaying negative emotions in the workplace, and Black men are burdened by the false stereotype that they are predisposed to anger. We're not talking here about moments of prudent self-censorship, which sometimes can't be divorced from a larger context of bias or low psychological safety. Instead, we're talking about inauthenticity as a strategy, a way of navigating the workplace. If this is how you operate, you're dealing with an authenticity wobble.

In our experience, although withholding your true self may sometimes help you solve problems in the short term, it puts an artificial cap on trust and, by extension, on your ability to lead. When people sense that you're concealing the truth or being less than authentic, they're far less willing to make themselves vulnerable to you in the ways that leadership demands.

We've observed the cost of inauthenticity up close in the performance of diverse teams. Diversity can be a tremendous asset in today's marketplace, and the companies that get it right often enjoy powerful competitive tailwinds. But this advantage isn't automatic. Simply populating your team with diverse perspectives and experiences doesn't always translate into better performance. In fact, the uncomfortable truth is that diverse teams can underperform homogenous teams if they're not managed actively for differences among members. That is due in part to a phenomenon called the common information effect, which works like this: As human beings, we tend to focus on the things we have in common with other people. We tend to seek out and affirm our shared knowledge, because it confirms our value and kinship with the group. Diverse teams, by definition, have less common information readily available to them to use in collective decision-making.

Consider two teams of three people, one in which the three members are different from one another, and the other in which they're similar. If both teams are managed in exactly the same way—if they simply follow the same best practices in group facilitation, for example—the homogenous team is likely to perform better. No amount of feedback or number of trust falls can overcome the strength of the common information effect.

But the effect only holds if people wobble on authenticity. When they choose to bring their unique selves to the table—that is, the parts of themselves that are different from other people—they can create an unbeatable advantage by expanding the amount of information the team can access. The result is an inclusive team that's likely to outperform (by a long shot) both homogenous teams and diverse teams that aren't actively managed for inclusion. (See the exhibit "Trust, diversity, and team performance.")

This expansion of knowledge and its obvious benefits rely on the courage of authenticity wobblers. We know how difficult sharing who we really are can be, and we also know that it's sometimes too much to ask. But if we regularly give in to the pressure to hold back our unique selves, then we suppress the most valuable parts of ourselves. Not only do we end up concealing the very thing the world needs most from us—our differences—but we also make it harder for people to trust us as leaders.

Here's the reason to care, even if you don't see yourself as different: All of us pay the price of inauthentic interactions, and all of us have a better chance of thriving in inclusive environments where authenticity can flourish. Gender bias, in other words, is not just a woman's problem. Systemic racism is not just an African American or Latinx problem. It's our shared moral and organizational imperative to create workplaces where the burdens of being different are shouldered by all of us. After all, we will all benefit wildly from eliminating them.

Trust, diversity, and team performance

Diversity doesn't automatically confer advantages in decision-making. In fact, if diverse teams aren't managed actively for inclusion, they can underperform homogenous ones. That's because shared knowledge is key in decision-making, and diverse teams, by definition, start out with less of it. But if you create conditions of trust that allow diverse team members to bring their unique perspectives and experiences to the table, you can expand the amount of knowledge your team can access—and create an unbeatable advantage.

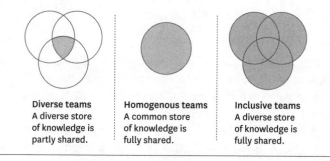

Diverse teams
A diverse store of knowledge is partly shared.

Homogenous teams
A common store of knowledge is fully shared.

Inclusive teams
A diverse store of knowledge is fully shared.

One of the lessons we've learned in our work with organizations is that creating spaces where authenticity can thrive is not as hard as it may seem. It is an urgent, achievable goal that requires far less audacity than disrupting industries or growing complex organizations—things leaders do every day with deep conviction in the outcomes. If all of us take responsibility for creating companies where difference can thrive, and all of us take responsibility for showing up in them authentically, then our chances of achieving true inclusion—and building high levels of trust—start to look pretty good.

So pay less attention to what you think people want to hear and more attention to what you need to say to them. Reveal your full humanity to the world, regardless of what your critics say. And while you're at it, take exquisite care of people who are different from you, confident in the knowledge that their difference is the very thing that could unleash your potential and your organization's.

In Myself I Trust

We've argued that the foundation of empowerment leadership is getting other people to trust you. That's certainly true, but there's one last thing you need to know. The path to empowerment leadership doesn't begin when other people start to trust you. It begins when you start to trust yourself.

To be a truly empowering leader, you need to take stock of where you wobble not only in your relationships with others but also in your relationship with yourself. Are you being honest with yourself about your ambitions, or are you ignoring what really excites and inspires you? If you're hiding something from yourself, you've got an authenticity problem you need to address. Do you acknowledge your own needs and attend properly to them? If not, you've got to adopt a more empathetic posture toward yourself. Do you lack conviction in your own ideas and ability to perform? If so, you've got some logic issues to work out.

Doing this work is important as a leader, for an arguably obvious reason. If you don't trust yourself, why should anybody else trust you?

A Campaign to Rebuild Trust

Let's now return to Uber. When we began working with the company, it was certainly wobbling—so much so that we diagnosed it as "a hot mess."

What was going on?

Consider the basic trust-related facts. There's no question that Uber had empathy problems. The company's focus on growth at all costs meant that relationships with stakeholders, particularly drivers and employees, needed real attention. Riders also needed to be assured that their safety wouldn't come second to the company's financial performance. Additionally, despite its disruptive success, Uber hadn't answered questions about the long-term viability of its business model or about whether its managers had the skills to lead an organization of its expansive scale and scope. These were unaddressed logic problems. Finally, the company's war-room mentality was undermining its authenticity. In the "us versus them" culture at Uber, people were skeptical that they were getting the full story.

By the time Frances began working with Kalanick, he had already begun making changes to steady the company's trust wobbles. He had hired Eric Holder, for example, who had served as U.S. attorney general under President Obama, to lead a rigorous internal investigation into harassment and discrimination—and when Holder made a sweeping set of recommendations, Kalanick took action to implement them. The company was also on the verge of rolling out new driver-tipping functionality, which would go on to generate $600 million in additional driver compensation in the first year of its launch. New safety features were in development, too, designed to give both drivers and riders additional tools to protect themselves.

Kalanick didn't get the chance to see most of these initiatives to completion, at least not from the CEO chair. In June 2017, he was forced out as CEO, although he retained his board seat and an equity stake in the company until December 2019, when he gave both up. He was ultimately replaced by Dara Khosrowshahi, the former Expedia CEO, who had a track record of effective leadership at the helm of young companies.

Frances soon began working with Khosrowshahi to continue the campaign to rebuild trust internally. Together they led an effort to rewrite the company's cultural values, one that invited input from all 15,000 employees on the principles that they wanted Uber to live by. The new motto they settled on was "We do the right thing. Period." Other early trust wins for Khosrowshahi included strengthening relationships with regulators and executing a logic-driven focus on the services and markets that were most defensible.

Most of the work we did during this period was aimed at rebuilding trust at the employee level. Some things were easy to identify and fix, like ratcheting down the widespread, empathy-pulverizing practice of texting during meetings about the other people in the meeting, a tech-company norm that shocked us when we first experienced it. We introduced a new norm of turning off all personal technology and putting it away during meetings, which forced people to start making eye contact with their colleagues again.

Other challenges were harder to tackle, like the need to upskill thousands of managers. Our take was that Uber had underinvested in its people during its period of hypergrowth, leaving many managers unprepared for the increasing complexity of their jobs. We addressed this logic wobble with a massive infusion of executive education, using a virtual classroom to engage employees in live case discussions—our pedagogy of choice—whether they were in San Francisco, London, or Hyderabad. Although our pilot program was voluntary and classes were sometimes scheduled at absurdly inconvenient times, 6,000 Uber employees based in more than 50 countries each participated in 24 hours of instruction over the course of 60 days. It was an extraordinary pace, scale, and absorption of management education.

The curriculum gave people tools and concepts to develop quickly as leaders while flipping a whole lot of upside-down communication triangles. Employees gained the skills not only to listen better but also to talk in ways that made it easier to collaborate across business units and geographies. Frances went out in the field, visiting key global offices in her first 30 days on the job, carving out protected spaces to listen to employees and communicate leadership's commitment to building a company worthy of its people. At a time when many employees were conflicted about their Uber affiliations, Frances made it a point to wear an Uber T-shirt every day until the entire company was proud to be on the payroll.

Within a year, Uber was less wobbly. There were still problems to be solved, but indicators such as employee sentiment, brand health, and driver compensation were all heading in the right direction, and the march toward an IPO began in earnest. Good people were deciding to stay with the company, more good people were joining, and, in what had become our favorite indicator of progress, an increasing number of Uber T-shirts could now be spotted on city streets. It was all a testament to the talent, creativity, and commitment to learning at every level of the organization—and to the new foundation of trust that Kalanick and Khosrowshahi had been able to build.

Originally published in May–June 2020. Reprint R2003H

Cultural Innovation

by Douglas Holt

BUILDING THE NEXT billion-dollar innovation is an irresistible goal. To get a leg up, many companies now emulate the innovation model perfected in the tech sector. Procter & Gamble, for example, pursues what it calls *constructive disruption*. The company has designed its innovation process like a start-up's, with a venture lab that pulls in tech entrepreneurs and a lean probe-and-learn prototyping process.

That approach is not working. The reality is that in most consumer markets, innovation is a slow, incremental grind—extending master brands, adding a new bell or whistle, tweaking a formula. P&G's star innovations—such as a smart Pampers diaper that signals when a change is needed—aren't exactly threatening to become the next billion-dollar product.

And when companies do swing for the fences, they rarely achieve good results. Take Coca-Cola, which has long prioritized building a business in coffee. After years of research and testing, the company bet big on two innovations—Far Coast Coffee (a retail chain premised on sustainability) and Coca-Cola BläK (Coke mixed with coffee). Both ideas failed badly, so the company eventually bought Costa Coffee, a British coffeehouse chain, at a steep price: $5 billion.

This problem is not an organizational one. Companies struggle because they put all their chips on one innovation paradigm— what I call *better mousetraps*. As Ralph Waldo Emerson noted long ago, "Build a better mousetrap, and the world will beat a path to your door." This is innovation as conceived by engineers and economists—a race to create the killer value proposition. It wins on functionality, convenience, reliability, price, or user experience. Better-mousetraps innovation is often the right bet if you're a tech company. Thousands of experts, seminars, and boot camps provide advice to help you on your way. But what about companies that operate in markets where new technology is less consequential or impossible to defend? For many of them, confronted with a pattern of poor return on investment, chasing better mousetraps seems like an exhausting and expensive matter of running in place.

Fortunately, building better mousetraps is not the only way to innovate. In consumer markets, innovation often proceeds according to a logic I call *cultural innovation*. Think of Starbucks, Patagonia, Jack Daniel's, Ben & Jerry's, and Vitaminwater. Remember, innovation is in the eye of the beholder. When those brands broke through, consumers viewed them as major innovations, although a better-mousetraps perspective would reject that assessment. In each case people responded to the brand's ideology—a reimagining of the category that transformed the value proposition. Cultural innovations are embodied in distinctive products or services, to be sure, but also in founders' speeches, packaging, ingredients, retail design, media coverage, and even philanthropy.

The result? Those brands don't compete in the value-proposition race, trying to lead the category as it's currently defined; they play a different game. Better-mousetraps innovation is guided by quantitative ambitions: Outdo your competitors on existing notions of value. Cultural innovation operates according to qualitative ambitions: Change the understanding of what is considered valuable.

I've spent the past 20 years researching and advising organizations on numerous cultural innovations. My work reveals the strategic principles that allow companies to pursue them—principles completely different from those used to build better mousetraps.

Ford Reinvents the Family Car

Buying a sport utility vehicle would have been an oddball idea for American middle-class families as late as 1989, but by 1995 the SUV was their unquestionable favorite, thanks largely to the Explorer—the

Idea in Brief

The Context

Most companies take a "better mousetraps" approach to innovation, improving a product's functionality—with only average results.

A Different Approach

A few take a cultural innovation approach instead, first identifying a weakness in the existing category

and then reinventing the category's ideology and symbolism.

The Results

The Ford Explorer, for example, replaced the boring "mom mobile" minivan as America's favorite family car with a promise of excitement, adventure, and glamour—even though the SUV wasn't a technically superior vehicle.

pioneering vehicle that earned Ford roughly $30 billion in operating profit over its first decade. A spartan enclosed truck, the Explorer was yanked from its traditional role as functional transport on farms and ranches to become the aspirational choice of suburban families for commuting, delivering youngsters to school, and heading out to the mall. It succeeded wildly despite violating the rules of better mousetraps at every turn. It was a classic cultural innovation, targeting a fatal flaw in the family car culture of that era.

The modern station wagon was a staple of the postwar nuclear-family ideal. All the major makes and models competed within this culture of suburban functionality. In the 1980s minivans rapidly replaced station wagons, winning on important benefits—plenty of seats, great storage, easy entrance and egress—that allowed families to haul kids and their friends around town and on summer trips.

The minivan's pragmatic design and ubiquity created a big symbolic problem. Vehicles are judged as much for the identity they project as for function: Status, sophistication, and masculinity all play a role in creating "premium" cars, which at the time were predominantly imports. Minivans came to represent the quotidian life of suburban parents, mocked as the centerpiece of a boring existence organized by "mom mobile" routines. Parents began to yearn for a car that would replace this stigma with an aspirational identity.

In the 1980s the Reagan-era revival of America's frontier ideology, which championed rugged individualists taming wild nature, inspired a critical mass of urban and suburban residents to reimagine the family car as a swashbuckling vehicle for off-road adventures. The offerings at the time were a poor fit for families: The Jeep Cherokee (XJ) and Chevy's massive Suburban were rough-driving trucks that lacked the amentities of passenger cars. The Ford Bronco and the Chevy S-10 Blazer offered only two doors. Nonetheless, many families were willing to forgo the minivan's creature comforts for the symbolic value that trucks bestowed. It took the incumbent automakers the better part of a decade to engage with this opportunity. They were lucky to be in an industry with very high barriers to entry; otherwise they would no doubt have been beaten to market by a challenger brand.

Eventually the big three domestic truck players—Ford, General Motors, and Chrysler Jeep—raced to bring a comfortable, luxuriously equipped four-door SUV to market. The winner would be the brand that managed to seduce parents into thinking about family cars in a new way. Jeep had the initial advantage, given its potent off-road pedigree, and its new Grand Cherokee, launched soon after the Explorer, won many plaudits. However, Jeep's idea of a family SUV was a straight take on the frontier-adventure myth, showcasing performance on wilderness outings—a myth better aimed at young single men than at upscale families.

The Explorer was launched with advertisements that dramatized a new ideal of family life, rejecting the dull suburban minivan. Ford made two crucial changes to the frontier-adventure myth, both of which connected powerfully with parents. Instead of Jeep's macho excursions, the company offered a vision of families communing in the wilderness. Ads showed them whisking off to remote places in an Explorer to make memories while gathering under the stars, kids happily trading in their tech for spiritual contentment. And parents who owned an Explorer got to have a life too. Ads showed them escaping on urban adventures—eating at boutique restaurants or attending the theater. They might live in the suburbs, but they could still enjoy a cosmopolitan life.

Families flocked to the Explorer. Sure, most of the time they were still hauling groceries and dropping kids off at soccer practice, just as they would have done with a minivan. But they were buying into a myth. Driving an Explorer allowed them to feel they'd finally escaped the world of mom mobiles for a more adventurous life.

In the postwar era, safety was a modest concern, despite Ralph Nader's best efforts. Even getting people to use seat belts was a challenge. By the early 1990s, though, car safety had captured the public's imagination owing to two big better-mousetraps innovations—airbags and antilock brakes—that were promoted heavily in auto advertising and the media.

Ford discovered early on that people believed that the huge size and weight of SUVs made them uniquely safe and that their off-road capabilities meant they were especially skid-resistant in bad weather. So the company crafted a sales pitch to reinforce that perception. The car's elevated seats conferred a feeling of power and invincibility, particularly for women. When couples came to a dealership, the salesperson would ask the woman to test-drive the Explorer so that she could appreciate the feeling of safety from the high perch. Ford was able to persuade customers that they were buying the safest car on the road.

The Explorer was a great success, comparable to celebrated Silicon Valley innovations in terms of its market impact and profitability. Yet its breakthrough is incomprehensible when viewed through the lens of better mousetraps. The vehicle was not an engineering advance—quite the opposite. It relied on dated technology. Explorers accelerated lethargically. They were top-heavy and cornered poorly. They cost a lot and were far more expensive to maintain than minivans. And they were gas-guzzlers that generated enormous increases in CO_2. But families were willing to pay near-luxury prices because the SUV perfectly addressed the symbolic problem in the market's status quo.

The Cultural Innovation Model

Let's look at a second case—Blue Buffalo dog food—to recognize the key steps in cultural innovation and to explain why incumbents often fail at it.

For decades Nestlé Purina, Mars, and Procter & Gamble dominated the profitable U.S. dog food category with powerful brands, distribution muscle, strong R&D, and big marketing budgets. Yet all three were beaten badly by Blue Buffalo, a tiny start-up, which was so successful that General Mills eventually bought it for $8 billion, while Procter & Gamble threw in the towel and sold its entire pet food division to Mars for less than $3 billion. Blue Buffalo bested the established brands by reinventing dog food culture. Here's how.

Step 1. Deconstruct the category's culture

Markets are belief systems embraced by those who participate in a category: companies, consumers, and the media. To understand your category's culture, think like a sociologist. Step back and make the familiar strange. What are the category's taken-for-granted organizing principles? What is the dominant ideology?

Before Purina launched the modern industrial dog food category, in the 1920s, most American families fed their dogs table scraps. Purina's standardized extruded kibble made inroads with consumers, and by the postwar era the company had adopted the mass-marketing techniques pioneered by food manufacturers such as Kraft and General Mills. Its ads featured heart-tugging images of cute dogs and their loving owners. The implicit message was "Purina is the biggest, best-known dog food company, so of course you can trust us to make food that will keep your dog healthy and energetic." Ingredients were rarely mentioned.

The category's first cultural innovation came in the 1970s, on the heels of media hype about scientific findings that certain vitamins and superfoods could keep people healthy. (Fiber and antioxidants were hot topics.) Cultural innovators, led by Hill's Science Diet and Iams, championed a new, scientific dog food ideology. The companies produced separate products for the various stages of a dog's life. Marketing featured veterinarians announcing cutting-edge formulas based on the best nutritional science. These products were sold in vets' offices—the ultimate sign of medical credibility. Purina launched a fast-follower grocery brand, Purina ONE, with ads featuring scientists in lab coats and packaging full of medical terminology.

These new brands taught owners to value dog food primarily for its nutritional benefits and offered them a scientific lexicon that "proved" quality nutrition. They encouraged owners to view the making of pet food as a complex scientific endeavor. The ingredients, however, remained hidden in small print.

Step 2. Identify the Achilles' heel

Categories' cultures eventually develop a fatal flaw, and cultural innovators pinpoint the emerging vulnerabilities. Throughout the early 2000s America's industrial-scientific food culture was subject to damning critiques in the media and by dozens of insurgent anti-industrial food movements. Dog owners began to feel similar concerns; they questioned whether those bags of kibble made by big companies were actually good for their pets. Then, in 2007, thousands of dogs and cats died after eating contaminated pet food. The media reported that one ingredient, wheat gluten contaminated with melamine, was bulk-sourced from China. Owners had had no idea that they were feeding their dogs wheat gluten or that it was imported from China. They began to take far more interest in the actual ingredients of dog food.

Step 3. Mine the cultural vanguard

Category transformations are usually prefigured by ideas and practices worked out at the margins. When cracks form in a category's culture, a *cultural vanguard* often appears before big companies show up. Innovators study the vanguard closely, and even participate in it, to find a strategic direction for their challenger ideology and the symbols required to bring it to life.

A small "natural" dog food subculture, separate from the national brands, had developed in prior decades. Alternative-health companies and their avid customers believed that healthful dog food should emulate what dogs ate before they became domesticated. The subculture's brands, which were sold in boutiques and natural-foods stores, were very expensive and marketed to niche customers. They made little effort to win converts from the big industrial-scientific brands.

A cultural innovation framework

Blue Buffalo upended industry giants like Purina and P&G by reconfiguring the category's ideology, using potent symbols. As a result, it transformed the value proposition for dog food.

Conventional dog food culture

Ideology
→ Industrial-scientific nutrition
→ Trust corporate scientific expertise to formulate nutritious food; don't worry about ingredients

Symbols
→ Ads showing happy dogs with their owners
→ Nutrition jargon
→ "Scientific" claims
→ Big national brands

The value proposition
Health: The most nutritious dog food is made by big corporations with scientific expertise
Identity: I'm a caring owner who buys the best food for my dog's health

Cultural disruption
Achilles' heel emerges
→ Industrial ingredients exposed as a health risk; melamine scare
→ Am I feeding my dog unhealthful food?

Cultural vanguard
→ Natural-foods subculture

Challenger dog food culture

Ideology
→ Preindustrial ancestral diet
→ Feed your pet the same foods that keep your family healthy

Symbols
→ Ads revealing inferior industrial ingredients
→ Plain package (no owner + pet)
→ Number one ingredient: real meat
→ No fillers, no meat by-products, no artificial ingredients
→ LifeSource Bits
→ Small family company

The value proposition
Health: Nutritious dog food is like human food but in a convenient, nonperishable form
Identity: To be a credibly caring owner, I need to upgrade to ingredients that I'd feed my family

The brands lionized whole ingredients and transparent supply chains. They were all about real meat, poultry, and fish, along with whole-food carbohydrates (sweet potatoes, rice), and they fastidiously avoided anything artificial. The subculture encouraged customers to beware of "fillers" (processed starches such as corn, wheat, and soy) and meat by-products. Their packaging highlighted ingredients rather than happy dogs and loving owners.

Step 4. Create an ideology that challenges the Achilles' heel

Cultural innovators source materials from the vanguard to build a new brand concept. The natural-foods subculture's ideology was hidden: Alternative-health zealots talked to one another and used rhetoric aimed at the already converted. Blue Buffalo, which was founded in 2002 by a Connecticut family that had become obsessed with the link between pet diet and health after their Airedale terrier (named Blue) died of cancer, acted as the subculture's proselytizer. The brand challenged the weak assumption that anchored the industrial-scientific ideology—that kibble was surely nutritious, even though owners had no idea what the compressed brown pellets were made from. In doing so, it created a litmus test for responsible dog ownership.

Blue Buffalo pushed owners to evaluate dog food as *food*. Those other kibble brands were full of industrial products that pet owners would never eat. People needed to take control and make sure their dog food contained healthful ingredients, no different from what they'd feed their families. Blue Buffalo's pet food was made with the same ingredients as a good human diet, so by switching brands, owners could ditch their newfound guilt and claim an enlightened identity—they really did feed their dogs nutritious food.

Step 5. Showcase symbols that dramatize the ideology

Cultural innovations are brought to life by a combination of symbols that dramatize them in the most compelling manner. They select symbols from the marketing mix that work together, attack the Achilles' heel, and draw a clear contrast with the category's dominant culture.

Blue Buffalo leveraged the leading symbols of the natural-foods subculture and created additional symbols to illustrate the notion that Blue Buffalo was, in effect, the same healthful food that owners themselves ate, converted into a compact, convenient, nonperishable form. The company repurposed the subculture's four foundational claims—real meat is the number one ingredient, no meat by-products, no fillers, nothing artificial—and used them in dozens of low-budget ads, produced to look like documentaries: Owners gathered in a living room, comparing notes on their preferred dog foods. Some were taken aback to read that their favorite brand contained "chicken by-product," while Blue Buffalo users proudly proclaimed that the first ingredient in theirs was deboned chicken. The company taught owners to read the label the next time they considered buying a bag of kibble.

And Blue Buffalo developed its own mini-kibble: LifeSource Bits—small, dark-purple (rather than brown) balls made with superfoods such as blueberries, flaxseed, cranberries, and kelp. The company pushed owners to draw a connection between what their families ate to avoid chronic disease and what would give their dogs the same kind of protection.

As Blue Buffalo's challenge worked its magic, millions of owners decided to spend far more on dog food to avoid guilt. They bought into an entirely new value proposition: a new nutritional benefit (healthful dog food contains the same ingredients that healthful human food does) and a new identity benefit (switching to Blue Buffalo proved that they were truly caring owners).

Why Incumbent Counterattacks Failed

Despite the company's strategic brilliance, Blue Buffalo should never have been able to build a business that was worth $8 billion. The three incumbents completely dominated the market and should have prevailed over the upstart. All three invested heavily in new brands and line extensions, but they struck out because, working with a better-mousetraps mindset, they misunderstood the nature of Blue Buffalo's cultural innovation.

Iams: Cultural incoherence

P&G believed that Blue Buffalo was gaining ground by making a big deal of a simple "new and improved" ingredients claim. The company assumed that if it matched those ingredients with a line extension, owners would choose the trusted brand over Blue Buffalo. So P&G launched Iams Healthy Naturals, featuring two of Blue Buffalo's ingredients claims (no fillers, no artificial ingredients), with a big ad campaign and promotions. When that attempt failed, the company tried a more expensive iteration, Iams Naturals, which had meat as the number one ingredient. But to no avail.

What went wrong? Both products relied on brand names that tried to knit together the dominant industrial-scientific ideology (which Iams had championed for decades) with the natural dog food subculture—and the result was culturally incoherent. Iams came off as an impostor. It didn't help that the company's advertising campaigns used exactly the same trope (loving owner playing with energetic pet) that industrial-scientific brands had relied on for 40 years instead of showcasing ingredients, a key concern in the natural pet food subculture. P&G unwittingly sabotaged its rebuttal with its confused symbolism.

Purina: Purpose gone awry

Purina, too, launched a line extension—Purina ONE Beyond—to defend against Blue Buffalo. The effort led with not one but two industrial-scientific brand names (Purina and ONE), inadvertently signaling to consumers that this was not a credible natural dog food.

In addition, the company (which fancied purpose-driven branding at the time) decided to tie Beyond to a purpose. It knew from trends research that upscale owners favored green products, so it decided that Beyond would be the dog food that helped save the planet. An anthemic launch ad, depicting a glowing field, proclaimed, "We believe together we can make the world a better place one pet at a time." The problem was that environmental sustainability had nothing to do with Blue Buffalo's challenge, which centered on nutrition and health. Dog owners simply ignored Beyond.

Mars: A mismanaged acquisition

Incumbents' standard response when threatened by cultural innovation is to buy the threatening company or a close competitor. In 2007 Mars did just that by acquiring Nutro, a strong brand in the natural pet food subculture and a credible challenger to Blue Buffalo. That was a promising move. To make it work, though, Mars would have had to shift Nutro marketing to attack industrial dog food, copying Blue Buffalo. It's unlikely that Mars ever considered that move, which would have meant attacking its biggest brand, Pedigree. Instead managers did just the opposite: They converted Nutro to a mass-marketing approach using ads little different from those of Iams.

P&G, Purina, and Mars never understood that they were fighting an existential battle to sustain their brands' authority as experts on healthful, nutritious dog food—not just racing to clean up their ingredients panels. As a result, Blue Buffalo convinced millions of dog owners that a product once viewed as a fussy extravagance was actually a necessity for people who truly loved their dogs.

Stuck in the Better-Mousetraps Mindset

Cultural innovation has often been an entrepreneur's gambit. Even when incumbents happen upon extraordinary cultural opportunities that should be easy to spot and straightforward to execute on, they fail time and again. If companies are to succeed at cultural innovation, they need to avoid three pitfalls.

Working eternally in the present

Even if they don't think in such terms, companies are masters of their category's existing culture. They have to be to excel at their current business. Their metrics and planning focus on it. As a result, managers come to perceive the category as an immutable reality, even though it's actually built on a fragile consensus. If you're trapped in the present tense, it is extremely difficult to examine the category from the outside and identify its emerging flaws. These ideological blinders explain why hundreds of highly trained professionals at the biggest pet food companies responded inadequately when Blue Buffalo attacked their billion-dollar businesses.

Being wedded to a product's features

The better-mousetraps paradigm assumes that a product's features are objective characteristics that consumers value. As a result, products are construed in building-block terms—as stacks of features that together create a value proposition. Innovation, then, requires improvements to particular features that consumers value. But features aren't just building blocks— they can be malleable cultural symbols of an ideology. The incumbent dog food companies assumed that Blue Buffalo was simply offering trendy new ingredients claims. But in fact those claims became "evidence" in Blue Buffalo's whistleblower project, revealing that owners had been hoodwinked by the industrial-scientific brands.

Ignoring the value of identity

The better-mousetraps paradigm views innovations as great functional achievements, but that overlooks a critical component of many innovations: bolstering aspects of consumers' identity. Ford, as we have seen, persuaded customers that they could trade in the dreary suburban minivan lifestyle for outdoor adventure and sophisticated city excursions. Blue Buffalo consumers traded up to garner status as enlightened dog owners.

In 1995 Clay Christensen introduced one of the most influential ideas in business: disruptive innovation. He famously asked why great companies fail when they're doing everything right. Christensen's answer: Incumbents focus on serving the most-demanding customers with the best products because margins are high. So entrants provide simple, cheap, "underperforming" solutions to low-end niches. Incumbents tend to ignore segments with poor margins and "inferior" products until it's too late. If one were to turn Christensen's advice into a mantra, it might be "Think like a cheapskate."

But that's not the only innovator's dilemma. Great companies are also disrupted by innovations that don't involve new technologies; a cheap, low-performance product; or a price-sensitive target. Incumbents are so intent on winning the category as it's currently defined that they fail to identify cracks in its foundation. Cultural innovators outmaneuver them because they look for opportunities to blow up the dominant ideology in favor of a new regime. So for incumbents to innovate, they'll need to adopt a second mantra: "Think like a cultural entrepreneur."

Originally published in September–October 2020. Reprint R2005J

The Rules of Co-opetition

by Adam Brandenburger and Barry Nalebuff

THE MOON LANDING just over 50 years ago is remembered as the culmination of a fierce competition between the United States and the USSR. But in fact, space exploration almost started with cooperation. President Kennedy proposed a joint mission to the moon when he met with Khrushchev in 1961 and again when he addressed the United Nations in 1963. It never came to pass, but in 1975 the Cold War rivals began working together on Apollo-Soyuz, and by 1998 the jointly managed International Space Station had ushered in an era of collaboration. Today a number of countries are trying to achieve a presence on the moon, and again there are calls for them to team up. Even the hypercompetitive Jeff Bezos and Elon Musk once met to discuss combining their Blue Origin and SpaceX ventures.

There is a name for the mix of competition and cooperation: *co-opetition*. In 1996, when we wrote a book about this phenomenon in business, instances of it were relatively rare. Now the practice is common in a wide range of industries, having been adopted by rivals such as Apple and Samsung, DHL and UPS, Ford and GM, and Google and Yahoo.

There are many reasons for competitors to cooperate. At the simplest level, it can be a way to save costs and avoid duplication of effort. If a project is too big or too risky for one company to manage, collaboration may be the only option. In other cases one party is better at doing A while the other is better at B, and they can trade skills. And even if one party is better at A and the other has no better B to offer, it may still make sense to share A at the right price.

Co-opetition raises strategic questions, however. How will the competitive dynamics in your industry change if you cooperate—or if you don't? Will you be able to safeguard your most valuable assets? Careful analysis is required. In this article we'll provide a practical framework for thinking through the decision to cooperate with rivals.

What Is Likely to Happen If You Don't Cooperate?

If a cooperative opportunity is on the table, start by imagining what each party will do if it's *not* taken. What alternative agreements might the other side make, and what alternatives might you pursue? If you don't agree to the deal, will someone else take your place in it? In particular, will the status quo still be an option?

Let's start with a simple example. Honest Tea (which one of us cofounded) was approached by Safeway supermarkets to make a private-label line of organic teas. The new line would undoubtedly eat into Honest Tea's existing Safeway sales. So even though the supermarket was offering a fair price, the deal would ultimately be unprofitable for Honest Tea.

However, if Honest Tea didn't cooperate, Safeway would surely find another supplier, such as rival tea maker Tazo. Honest figured that if it took the deal, it could design the new Safeway "O Organics" line to resemble the flavors and sweetness of Tazo's products and compete less against its own. If Honest had said no, Tazo would probably have said yes and targeted Honest's flavors, leading to the worst possible outcome. So Honest agreed to the deal.

Yet the company turned down a similar request from Whole Foods because the grocery chain insisted that the private line include a clone of Moroccan Mint, Honest's best-selling tea at the time. Honest didn't want to compete so directly against itself and believed that its rivals would have trouble copying the tea—which indeed turned out to be true.

Idea in Brief

The Context

The idea that competitors should sometimes cooperate with one another has continued to gain traction since it was initially explored in the 1990s.

The Issue

Even so, executives who aren't comfortable with "co-opetition" bypass promising opportunities.

A Framework for Action

Start by analyzing what each party will do if it doesn't cooperate and how that decision will affect industry dynamics. Sometimes cooperation is a clear win. Even if it isn't, it may still be preferable to not cooperating. But it's critical to try to figure out how to cooperate without losing your current advantages.

UPS had to think through a similar opportunity when DHL, which had acquired Airborne Express some years earlier and was suffering large losses, asked UPS to fly DHL's packages within the United States. UPS had the scale to make the service efficient (potentially saving DHL $1 billion a year) and was already providing a similar service to the U.S. Postal Service, so the opportunity appeared to be a profitable one that would allow UPS to rent out space on planes it was already flying.

That said, *not* cooperating might have been even more profitable in the long run. If DHL's continuing losses led to its exit, UPS stood to gain much of DHL's U.S. market share.

But if UPS turned the deal down, DHL might have offered it to FedEx. And if FedEx accepted it, DHL would still be in the market and UPS would have lost out on potential profits. So UPS agreed to DHL's proposal, announcing a deal in May 2008. (It turned out to be not enough to save DHL, which decided during the recession later that year to leave the market.)

In the tech industry, thinking through alternatives to a deal is complicated because companies have multiple relationships with one another. Samsung's decision about whether to sell Apple its new Super Retina edge-to-edge OLED screen for the iPhone X is a good example.

Samsung could have temporarily hurt Apple in the high-end smartphone market—where the Samsung Galaxy and iPhone compete—by not supplying its industry-leading screen. But Apple isn't the only rival Samsung has to worry about. In addition to being one of the world's largest phone manufacturers, Samsung is also one of the largest suppliers to phone manufacturers (including Apple, across several generations). If it hadn't provided its Super Retina display to Apple, Apple could have turned to LG (which supplies OLED screens for Google's Pixel 3 phones) or BOE (which supplies AMOLED screens for Huawei's Mate 20 Pro phones), strengthening one of Samsung's screen-technology competitors. Plus, Apple is well-known for helping its suppliers improve their quality. Cooperating with Apple meant that Samsung would get this benefit and that its screen-technology rivals would not. The fact that the deal would increase Samsung's scale and came with a big check attached—an estimated $110 for each iPhone X sold—ultimately tilted the balance toward cooperating.

It takes two to cooperate. Now let's look at the deal from Apple's perspective. Would it make Samsung a more formidable rival? It probably would: In the year prior to the iPhone X launch, revenue from Apple accounted for almost 30% of the Samsung display business, a division that generated $5 billion in profits. (Apple was also buying DRAM and NAND flash memory chips, batteries, ceramics, and radio-frequency-printed circuit boards from Samsung.) But for Apple, getting the best screen was worth bankrolling an already well-resourced rival—at least for a while.

The underlying economic reason that working together was advantageous to *both* sides was that Samsung had the best screen and Apple had a loyal customer base. Without cooperating, neither company could get the extra value from putting the superior screen on the new iPhone.

Will Cooperation Give Away Your Competitive Advantage?

Suppose you've analyzed the alternatives to cooperation and tentatively decided to move ahead. Doing so may mean sharing your special sauce. Then it might not be so special, and that could be a real problem. To get a read on the potential risk, figure out which of these four categories the deal falls into:

Neither party has a special sauce at risk, but the parties' combined ingredients create value

In this scenario neither side is giving anything away. A recent example is Apple and Google's decision to cooperate in creating contact-tracing technology for Covid-19. By sharing user location data across platforms, the two companies enabled governments and others to create effective notification apps. The circumstances here are exceptional, but it's not unusual for rivals to team up to set standards and create interoperability protocols and thereby create a bigger pie they can later fight over.

Both parties have a special sauce, and sharing puts them both ahead of their common rivals

In 2013, Ford and GM agreed to share transmission technologies. This made sense because they had complementary capabilities: Ford led in 10-speed transmissions, GM in nine-speed. The arrangement saved both money, had no significant strategic impact, and freed their engineers to work on next-generation electric vehicles, giving each company a leg up on other automakers.

There's a caveat here: Cooperation is more challenging if the playing field isn't level at the start. GM turned down an opportunity to collaborate with Ford on a next-generation diesel engine for super-duty pickup trucks. Though the potential cost savings were compelling, Ford already had a competitive advantage in the F-150's lightweight all-aluminum body, and GM feared that without differentiation between engines, Ford would have an unbeatable edge.

Sometimes, getting ahead of (or not falling behind) other rivals outweighs considerations of relative advantage. Autonomous driving technology, for instance, will be a key capability in the near future. Most automakers recognize that they won't be able to develop self-driving vehicles quickly or cost-effectively alone. That's why Ford invited Volkswagen to join its investment in Argo AI, an autonomous vehicle start-up. VW's $2.6 billion investment (along with its $500 million purchase of Ford's shares of the start-up) greatly reduced the drain on Ford's resources.

The deal also plays to each party's respective strength in getting regulatory approvals—Ford is strong in the United States, VW in Europe—significantly increasing the chance that Argo AI will be one of the platforms that gets worldwide approval. Ford also believed that if it didn't work with VW, VW would find another partner, which would decrease the chance that Argo AI would become one of the approved standards.

Because Ford's market share is greater than VW's in the United States and VW is ahead of Ford in Europe, it was a good bet that this partnership wouldn't change the balance of power between them. The focus was on elevating the pair relative to their many rivals.

One party has a strong competitive advantage, and sharing only heightens it; even so, less-powerful parties are willing to cooperate

Amazon gives rival sellers on Amazon Marketplace access to its customers and warehouses. Why? For starters, while it loses some direct business and the associated markup, it makes a commission on Marketplace sales. The net effect on profit depends on how the commission compares with the markup, and whether Amazon Marketplace (which accounts for $50 billion of the company's revenue) leads to an increase in the company's total volume.

Even if the net effect were negative, blocking rival sellers from its platform would push them to other sites that could compete with Amazon. More important, though, when Amazon shares its platform, it becomes a hub—the starting place for any search. It makes money when a person looking for a book or a computer cable comes to its site and purchases additional, higher-margin products like electronics or clothing. Amazon also learns about the customer's preferences and can use this data to offer better recommendations and more accurately identify which Amazon-branded products to offer. And finally, opening up Amazon Marketplace allows Amazon to operate more warehouses and increase shipping volume, thereby reducing shipping times and lowering overall costs.

But why do other merchants cooperate with Amazon? Each partner, acting individually, finds it more profitable, even necessary, to be part of the Amazon ecosystem. But it's a collective action problem: When the merchants all join its platform, they make Amazon a more formidable rival. Indeed, both the European Commission and the U.S. House Subcommittee on Antitrust, Commercial, and Administrative Law are investigating whether Amazon Marketplace is using its dominant position to undermine and compete unfairly with its merchant "partners."

One party shares its secret sauce to reach another's customer base, even though doing so carries risks for both parties
We saw this dynamic when Samsung shared its high-end screen with Apple. Google and Yahoo provide another example.

Google is better than any of its rivals at turning ads that appear alongside searches into clicks—that's its secret sauce. In 2008 it agreed to do ad placement for Yahoo. Google's technology would generate substantially more revenue per search for Yahoo, and sharing it was the quickest, surest way to extend its value to the market Google didn't already have. (In the short run, Google was unlikely to capture all of Yahoo's customers. By 2020, Yahoo's share of search was down to 1.6%, but that decline took a dozen years.)

The potential gains were enormous. Given Yahoo's then 17% share of the $9 billion market, a 50% to 60% revenue increase would create almost $1 billion in annual profits to be split between the two companies.

The deal did carry some risks for Google. It might have made Yahoo into a stronger competitor, but that possibility was less worrisome because Yahoo was already cash-rich owing to its stake in Alibaba. (More cash probably wasn't material to its competitive position.) Improved ad technology on Yahoo might have led some Google users to switch, but it seemed unlikely that better ads would cause a large number to do so. Perhaps the greatest risk was that Yahoo would learn the recipe for Google's special sauce—but Google never planned to hand over its algorithms.

The risks for Yahoo were bigger. Its capabilities might wither if it became dependent on Google's black box. Were the partnership to end, Yahoo would be further behind, perhaps dangerously so. Those risks were mitigated by Yahoo's plan to continue doing ad placement for its sites in Europe and thus maintain its own capabilities.

In the end the deal didn't materialize; the U.S. Department of Justice ruled against it on the grounds that it might leave Yahoo a weaker competitor in the future. (One of us helped defend the agreement.) But the economics were compelling. One year later, Yahoo made a deal with Microsoft to have Bing provide its search ads.

It isn't always possible to rent the sauce without giving away the recipe, however. Could the United States and China, for instance, cooperate on a mission to Mars? A seemingly insurmountable challenge is that it would involve sharing intellectual property that can't be recaptured. This is a particularly sensitive issue since space technology spills over to military applications.

How to Structure an Agreement

The parties have almost gotten to yes. They've identified a desirable opportunity and found a way to share their special sauce without giving away the recipe. The remaining task is to craft the agreement. Two issues are particularly challenging when a prospective partner is also a competitor: the scope of the deal and how the costs and benefits will be divided. (There may also be antitrust concerns; for more on those, see the sidebar "What About Antitrust Issues?")

Establishing scope and control

First the parties have to figure out how far to extend their cooperation, who is in charge, and how they might unwind their arrangement should it no longer make sense.

The simplest types of cooperation are limited and don't raise control issues. In some cases one party becomes a nonessential supplier to the other—as Honest Tea did with Safeway or as CBS did when it supplied the show *Dead to Me* to Netflix. In other cases the parties share costs but not proprietary knowledge. Rival television stations sometimes share camera crews, for instance, and rival breweries coordinate on recycling. Several museums in a city may

What About Antitrust Issues?

REGULATORS ARE NATURALLY SUSPICIOUS when rivals get together. Executives need to know which types of cooperation are permissible and which are not. Some antitrust violations are black-and-white: Businesses that coordinate to raise prices or divide up the market are engaged in collusion, pure and simple.

Regulators tend to take a more favorable view when businesses work together to reduce costs or expand demand. One good litmus test is to ask if customers will be better off as a result of the cooperation. For example, customers benefit if rivals partner to provide charging stations for electric cars. Similarly, supplying a rival tends to pass muster when it improves quality (as is the case when Samsung sells its Super Retina screens to Apple) and doesn't foreclose market entry to other players.

There is always the possibility that regulators will step in to nix a deal, as they did with Yahoo's 2008 agreement to have Google provide it with search ads. This is one of the challenges of co-opetition.

---

run an ad campaign or develop an all-access museum pass together. Generally these arrangements are easy to negotiate and can be unwound easily.

Agreements become challenging when one party has to cede control, however. Ford and GM's plan to share transmission technologies worked well at the R&D stage, but neither company was willing to give control of manufacturing to the other or even to a joint entity. Ford and GM could have written a contingent contract about who got what transmission production capacity when, but this would have been tricky since demand is variable and transmissions are mission-critical. Fortunately, the majority of the cost savings came from using common designs and common parts, so Ford and GM limited the agreement to those areas.

In other circumstances one party is in charge and the other party is protected by a contingent contract with performance guarantees and penalties for not hitting specific targets. This works well in situations where there are established performance benchmarks. The party in charge, the one providing the guarantees, doesn't have to be told what to prioritize; instead the right-sized penalties allow it to internalize decisions and make calls that optimize the combined outcome.

It's important to structure any agreement in such a way that one side doesn't become dependent on the other. Otherwise, the dependent party may be backed into a corner when it comes time to renegotiate the deal—or distressed when the deal ends. As noted earlier, this was one of the Justice Department's issues with the 2008 Google-Yahoo deal.

Dividing the pie

Cooperation is an overall win-win, but splitting the gains is a zero-sum game. The solution is relatively straightforward when there's an even trade, as when Ford and GM shared transmissions. It's harder if cooperation involves an uneven trade and payments are required.

Consider interairline agreements to help stranded passengers. For a long time it was customary for airlines to take care of one another's passengers in the event of a flight cancellation, or what the industry calls an IROP (irregular operation). Airlines paid a low IROP rate to secure a seat on another carrier.

Cooperation broke down in 2015 when Delta thought other airlines were getting the better end of the deal and proposed a steep increase in the IROP rate. Delta was taking five American Airlines passengers for each Delta passenger that American took. American declined to pay more, and the agreement ended.

The underlying problem was an uneven trade. With an even balance of trade, the IROP fare doesn't matter. When the trade is out of balance, the right price is what ensures a fair deal. An IROP fare that was Delta's cost of a seat (including forgone sales to displaced customers) plus half the value of American's gains (the savings on a hotel and meals and avoidance of the customer's ire) should have done the trick.

There might have been a way to save at least part of the deal without agreeing on price. Delta and American could have set up an agreement that guaranteed parity, trading seats on a one-for-one basis. If one airline had more cancellations and took more seats, the number of seats it got could be rationed going forward until things evened out.

The problem was ultimately resolved when the balance of trade was restored. After a series of computer outages and systemwide shutdowns, Delta found that it, too, needed some help. It renewed an agreement with American in 2018.

The challenges are greater when there are three or more parties to the deal and offsetting trades aren't possible. Take Ionity, a joint venture involving BMW, Daimler, Ford, Hyundai, Kia, and VW, which is building ultrafast electric-charging stations across Europe. The speed and cost-savings advantages from teaming up are enormous. Still, each partner has different geographical priorities, creating tensions over where to place the stations.

Splitting the massive price tag is even harder. It wouldn't work to divide the costs equally; the partners have significantly different shares of the market, and Kia, with its much smaller slice, would walk away. Costs could be split according to market share—but should market share be based on unit sales, dollar sales, profits, or even miles driven? Each party had its favorite answer.

In the end the six companies agreed that costs would be divided in proportion to current unit sales. A simple, albeit somewhat arbitrary, heuristic like that may be a practical way to get a cooperative venture off the ground.

Changing Minds

Cooperation with rivals also has an important emotional aspect. Some people are comfortable with the idea that there can be multiple winners, and some are not. As a result, co-opetition may end up being a strategy of last resort even in cases where it should be a first resort.

Apple was on the verge of failure in August 1997 when Steve Jobs was finally forced to confront the fact that Microsoft was not the enemy. Jobs later admitted that "if the game was a zero-sum game where for Apple to win, Microsoft had to lose, then Apple was going to lose." That change in perspective was hard for Apple loyalists to accept. When Jobs announced at the Macworld conference that Microsoft had invested $150 million in Apple, Bill Gates was booed.

Obvious opportunities for cooperation fall by the wayside when businesspeople don't focus on ensuring that all parties come out ahead. The world of check payments illustrates the problem.

Ever since printed checks were invented, more than 300 years ago, banks have needed a way to exchange those deposited by their account holders but written on other banks' accounts. The obvious solution was to establish a central clearinghouse. When the London banks failed to do this, the bank runners did it themselves. Instead of crisscrossing the city to exchange checks, they did an end run and all met at the Five Bells tavern. Some 50 years later the banks established the Bankers' Clearing House to do the same job.

In the modern era the U.S. Federal Reserve operated a system in which each bank would forward the paper checks it received to the Fed, which would then distribute them to the banks on which they were written. In 2001 some 40 billion checks were being flown around the country.

A logical alternative was to scan the checks and send digital images, thereby saving time and money. The challenge was that some of the small banks weren't set up to process digital images. Thus cooperation would further tilt the playing field. When the large banks didn't ensure that the small banks would also come out ahead, the small banks used their political power to block digital check clearing.

Then 9/11 forced the issue. With all planes grounded for over a week, checks were stranded and could not be cleared. At that point, the large banks finally agreed to ease the transition for small banks by having the Fed print the digital images and send the substitute checks to the small banks. In 2003 digital check clearing became established in law when Congress enacted the Check Clearing for the 21st Century Act.

It's also possible to work *around* mindsets. One solution is compartmentalization—both mental and actual. The Apple-Samsung deal, which happened during a billion-dollar legal battle between the two tech giants over patent infringements, was doubtless easier to arrange given that Samsung operates as three separate companies with three separate CEOs. Apple could cooperate with one autonomous part of Samsung while competing with and suing another.

For a similar reason, we think it was wise for Ford to keep Argo AI, the autonomous vehicle start-up, a separate company. It was psychologically and contractually easier to get VW to invest in an entity that was outside Ford. The external structure helps ensure that the two will be equals and also makes it easier to bring in future partners.

Ultimately, getting the right mindset requires choosing the right people. The executives we interviewed emphasized the need to staff the cooperating teams with people who are open to the dual mindset of co-opetition.

That isn't always easy, because people tend to think in either/or terms, as in either compete or cooperate, rather than compete *and* cooperate. Doing both at once requires mental flexibility; it doesn't come naturally. But if you develop that flexibility and give the risks and rewards careful consideration, you may well gain an edge over those stuck thinking only about competition.

We began this article with the missed opportunity for cooperation between the United States and the Soviet Union on a mission to the moon. Today the opportunities for countries to cooperate are even larger—from tackling Covid-19 and climate change to resolving trade wars. We hope that a better understanding of co-opetition will help businesses, managers, and countries find a better way to work and succeed together.

Originally published in January–February 2021. Reprint R2101C

Negotiating Your Next Job

by Hannah Riley Bowles and Bobbi Thomason

WHEN WE ASK PROFESSIONALS to describe a career negotiation, the first thing many people think of is bargaining with a hiring manager over an offer package. That scenario may spring to mind because compensation negotiations can be especially stressful and awkward and therefore become seared into our memories.

Although reaching agreement on pay and benefits is important, failure to think more broadly about your career could mean losing valuable opportunities for advancement. For instance, women are increasingly urged to negotiate for higher pay as a way to close the gender wage gap. However, studies have shown that women's "80 cents on the dollar" is explained more by differences in men's and women's career trajectories than by differential pay for doing the exact same job. Our research and our work coaching executives suggest that negotiating your role (the scope of your authority and your developmental opportunities) is likely to benefit your career more than negotiating your pay and benefits does. And at times of work-life conflict, negotiating your workload and the conditions that affect it (including your responsibilities, your location, and travel requirements) may be critical to remaining gainfully employed and moving forward professionally.

As with other dealmaking, career negotiations should not be solely about getting as much as you can. The best negotiators generate mutually beneficial solutions through joint problem-solving and creative trade-offs, along with compromise. Furthermore, negotiating the direction of your career typically involves multiple stakeholders—including those in your personal life as well as those at work.

We advise professionals to think strategically about not just *what* they might negotiate but *how*. That means going beyond planning what to say at the bargaining table; it requires keeping your eye on larger objectives, ensuring that you are negotiating with the right parties over the right issues, and preventing misunderstandings from derailing your requests or proposals because they are unconventional or potentially pathbreaking.

In the age of Covid-19, the time is ripe to improve your career negotiation skills. Many people are changing how they work (shifting to remote or flexible arrangements, for example), what they are working on (being redeployed or responding to new priorities), and with whom they're working (collaborating in new ways across functions and geographies). And transformations in our work lives are increasingly interlinked with transformations in our personal lives—whether that involves relocation decisions, periods of intense dedication to our jobs, or adapting to spikes in caregiving demands.

Drawing from a research project in which we collected thousands of stories from recent professional-school graduates, midlevel managers, and senior executives from seven global regions about how they advanced at pivotal points in their careers, we propose four steps for preparing for your career negotiations. They progress in a logical order, but you are likely to return to earlier steps as your analysis proceeds. For instance, you might start out intending to negotiate for one type of opportunity but discover that you're better off negotiating for a different type. Or you might initially conceive of a proposal to present to your boss but then come to understand that your boss is actually not the key stakeholder who needs to be persuaded. Particularly for a complex and protracted negotiation, you should continually refine your analysis as you gain information.

1. Start with Your Career Goals

In our experience, negotiators too often start their preparation focused on the opportunity right in front of them, such as a job offer, rather than on their ultimate work and life aspirations. As you enter

Idea in Brief

The Problem

In job negotiations, professionals too often focus on pay and benefits and fail to think more broadly about how the opportunity will fit into their long-term career goals.

The Way to Start

Work backward from your career objectives to define the next steps you want to take. Be mindful of whether you're proposing something standard, an unusual arrangement for yourself, or an idea that will change the organization.

The Negotiation

Make sure you have all the necessary information and aren't operating under false assumptions. Explain why your request is also in the other party's interest. Seek input and feedback from people who could be helpful, and enlist allies to support your proposal.

a period of change in your career, you should think about your short- and long-term aims and then map backward from those objectives to define the next steps you want to take. Don't forget to include quality-of-life considerations as well as professional ones. And be prepared to defer gratification if that's the right thing to do for the endgame.

Anya's story offers a cautionary tale. ("Anya" and all other individuals discussed in this piece are composites of case examples we studied.) When finishing her MBA program, she was evaluating two offers: one in consulting—the field she had previously worked in for several years—and one that would launch a new career in tech, which was what her heart truly desired. (Feeling torn between two industries is common in job searches.) The consulting firm was offering her more money and status than the tech company was— unsurprising, given her track record in consulting and her limited experience in tech (one summer internship). Focused on the terms of the offers, Anya started her negotiation preparation wondering if she should walk away from the tech company unless it matched the salary offered by the consulting firm.

Making compensation the deciding factor can be a mistake. If we'd been coaching Anya, we would have encouraged her to start with her career goal: transitioning out of consulting into tech. We would have encouraged her to compare the competing offers not only with each other but also against her vision of what she wanted to achieve in her first five years out of graduate school. Next we might have asked, "To improve the tech offer, what might you negotiate to fulfill your dream of a career in tech?" After all, her lifetime earning potential could be higher in that booming sector than in consulting. Perhaps she could accept the lower compensation but negotiate for an accelerated promotion track—a solution that might appeal to the tech company because it would not need to deviate from its compensation standards for MBA recruits.

Such longer-term thinking often pays off. In *Chasing Stars: The Myth of Talent and the Portability of Performance,* Boris Groysberg reports that the financial analysts who were most likely to retain their star status after moving to a new firm were those who had looked beyond pay and carefully researched whether the new firm would provide them with the organizational resources to excel. They understood that being successful in one setting doesn't guarantee success in another, so the compensation package was just one aspect of the job offer to consider. Our advice is to define from the start what you most want to achieve—whether that's being a top professional, making money, or living up to some other ideal—and then keep that goal in mind as your negotiation progresses.

2. Understand What You're Negotiating For

Career negotiations fall into three buckets. In *asking* negotiations, you propose something that's standard for someone in your role or at your level. In *bending* negotiations, you request a personal exception or an unusual arrangement that runs counter to typical organizational practice or norms (for example, a remote work setup or a promotion to a position for which you lack the conventional qualifications). And in *shaping* negotiations, you propose ways to play a role in changing your organizational environment or creating a new initiative (such as revamping the way a project is run or launching a new business unit). Depending on whether you are in an asking, a bending, or a shaping negotiation, you will need to vary your arguments to win your counterparts' support.

In asking situations, you must demonstrate that your request or proposal is reasonable because it fits with existing practices or norms—for example, a pay raise is warranted in light of an outside offer, or you deserve a promotion or a developmental opportunity because other employees with your track record or experience have received such rewards. Asking negotiations often arise in the context of routine conversations about role assignments. If you are asked to do work that would move you away from your career goals, see if there is room for negotiation. For instance, you might be able to explain why the proposed change in your role is not in the employer's interest: Perhaps it would hurt the performance of your team or damage the relationship with a high-value client. Another option is to agree to do the job for the sake of organizational needs in exchange for some other career-advancing opportunity. For example, you might say, "I will take on this role to help us out of the current crisis, but I would like to rotate into a job with more P&L responsibility after two years."

If you are in a bending negotiation—seeking some special exception or privilege—you need to keep your counterparts from doing what's easiest and simply saying, "No, that's not the way things are done around here." Justifying your request is particularly important if you are asking people to take a chance on you, such as putting you in a position for which you are not traditionally qualified.

Consider the case of Bela, who wanted to move from finance into a leadership role in IT as her company launched a digital transformation. The CIO considered her unqualified and seemed likely to dissuade the CEO from giving her the job. Bela came to realize that the CIO wanted someone more experienced to oversee the IT transition, in part because failure would reflect poorly on the CIO's own leadership. So she asked for a six-month trial while the CIO searched for a potential replacement. Bela explained why her deep knowledge of the company's financial systems and her track record managing cross-functional teams prepared her to succeed in this IT role or, at a minimum, keep the company on solid footing until she was replaced by a new hire.

Although any negotiation can backfire, bending negotiations are particularly risky because they may give the impression that you're a prima donna seeking special treatment or unwilling to pay your dues. Deborah Kolb, an expert in career negotiations, suggests a role-play exercise to mitigate this risk: List the reasons why your counterparts would support your proposal; then come up with a list of reasons why they might say no anyway—and your possible responses. Beyond strategizing to get past "no," we advise weighing the downstream career risks and benefits of entering into an exceptional or unconventional work arrangement.

Whereas asking and bending negotiations are focused solely on your personal career path, shaping negotiations center on proposals to change the path of your organization or working group. Because that commonly means seizing leadership opportunities, shaping negotiations typically involve more parties and the backing of allies.

Consider Samir's desire to lead a restructuring of his firm, which was run by an elite old guard that he saw as out of step with globally competitive business practices. Samir recognized that he needed to build a cross-generational coalition to support this change. As he made his case to key colleagues, he found allies among the veteran leaders who recognized that the firm's legacy would depend on retaining bold thinkers like him. He also found peers who appreciated his vision for growth. Finally, with his spouse's support, Samir worked out a plan to relocate internationally for another position if the firm rejected his proposal. He then began the negotiation process with confidence that he had enough buy-in within the firm to lead a transformational change, but also a satisfying alternative for himself and his family if that was not possible.

Organizations may be especially receptive to bending and shaping negotiations during challenging or fast-changing times, when people are looking for ways to adapt and innovate. For instance, in light of the Covid-19 pandemic and social distancing restrictions, many employees need to change the way they work. Their collective bending negotiations are a useful source of information and experimentation for organizations and individuals trying to figure out how to maintain high morale and productivity during the crisis.

Organizations are also welcoming shaping proposals from employees who have ideas about how to redeploy resources and open new markets in response to economic disruptions at home and abroad.

3. Reduce Ambiguity About What, How, and with Whom to Negotiate

No one would ever advise walking blind into a potential negotiation, but people do it all the time. One risk is that you'll "get Wahlberged," as the journalist Kate MacArthur put it, writing about how Mark Wahlberg negotiated a payment of $1.5 million to reshoot some scenes in a Hollywood film while his costar Michelle Williams accepted less than $1,000 for the same work. That case has been highlighted as an example of women's failure to negotiate, but the underlying problem was a lack of information on what was negotiable. Williams had been led to believe that all the actors on the reshoot were effectively donating their time to save the film after another costar was pulled from the cast.

Reducing ambiguity is particularly important for ensuring that people from underrepresented groups—oftentimes women and people of color—get a fair shake. Many organizations are moving to make their recruitment and promotion practices more transparent so that all candidates have access to the same information and opportunities. Increasing transparency is obviously the responsibility of organizations, but individuals can take action too.

As you prepare to negotiate, write down all the questions you have: *What is potentially negotiable? How should I negotiate? Who will be my counterparts, and what do they care about?* There are many sources for this type of information. Talent professionals, for example, will explain in general terms what is typically negotiable and how (although they usually won't reveal the specifics of any individual case). Some information is available online. A media or YouTube search can give you perspective on counterparts' points of view on strategic issues. A LinkedIn search can help you find professional contacts who may tell you more about a hiring manager or a department.

Although your personal and professional networks can be a valuable source of information, you should not rely on them alone to get an unbiased understanding of the situation. Think of a field in which men tend to be better paid than women. If women confer only with other women about customary salaries, and if men confer only with other men, women are likely to enter pay negotiations with lower expectations than men have—and to exit with worse outcomes.

Stretch your inquiry beyond your closest networks to ensure that you have the broadest information possible. Recently many people have been learning from how organizations in other industries or geographies are responding to the challenges presented by the Covid-19 pandemic. Better information helps generate innovative solutions; it can also help you make a persuasive case for managing your career the way you want to during these turbulent times.

4. Enhance Your Negotiations Through Relationships— and Vice Versa

As you aim to reduce ambiguity, you will undoubtedly think of people you might go to for information or advice. You might also think of others who could provide social support—those who would encourage and stand by you and give honest feedback if you are off track. Don't forget to identify potential advocates for your proposal. Who might be willing to speak up in favor of it? Who are your allies? Connecting with people who can be helpful is what we mean by enhancing your negotiations through relationships.

Consider the example of Brandon, an engineer who landed a job as a private equity associate after finishing business school. Lacking finance experience, he had been advised that his prospects of making partner were dim if he did not make a distinctive contribution. Brandon hoped to do that by arguing for the creation of a small fund to invest in marketable robotics projects—an underdeveloped growth area for the firm. Before negotiating to spearhead this initiative, he sought advice from his former robotics professor, who could spot weaknesses in his proposal and help him fix them. He also found a partner at the firm who agreed to let Brandon shadow him on tech company boards.

To build a coalition of support for what you hope to do, you might start off by trying something akin to the shuttle diplomacy used by negotiators of international affairs: Make the rounds of key stakeholders, talking with them individually to solicit their feedback and input. Shuttling is more time-consuming than calling a summit of all interested parties (a meeting to pitch your proposal). But it enables you to privately explore people's interests and concerns and to incorporate their ideas into your game plan. It also helps you predict how people will respond when it comes time for you to present a formal proposal.

If you're concerned that shuttling around might make you appear conniving or manipulative, then be transparent about it. Explain that you're seeking input on an idea you have, and meet early with people who might block your proposal if they felt you weren't consulting them. To broaden buy-in, you might also enlist others to help you get feedback, keeping in mind Harry Truman's words: "It is amazing what you can accomplish if you do not care who gets the credit."

Many of the negotiation cases we studied were rife with tales of conflict and resistance, but you needn't settle for compromises that leave both sides unhappy. The give-and-take that occurs when you're seeking a mutually beneficial deal can open your eyes to other perspectives, help you better understand your colleagues, and find ways of working together to create lasting solutions. In other words, career negotiations can enhance your working relationships—and we encourage you to strive for that outcome.

To generate goodwill and motivate agreement, we recommend that you explain to counterparts both why it is legitimate for you to be negotiating and how your proposal takes their interests into account. That's not always easy. For instance, we met one female executive who found out for the second time that a male subordinate was being paid more than she was. She probably wanted to say many things to senior leaders at her firm, but she chose the approach she knew would be most persuasive: "I know you are going to want to fix this, because it is inconsistent with company practices and values."

Or take the example of Sandra, who ran the U.S. division of a major business unit and wanted to globalize it. To achieve her aim, she had to make a strategic case for why globalization was in the company's best interest and why she was the right person to lead the initiative. Addressing the hopes and concerns of managers both at headquarters and in the non-U.S. business units required numerous rounds of conversation in which she seeded and got feedback on her ideas. Sandra told us: "Over time, the logic [for globalization and my leadership] became compelling."

The four steps outlined above take time to implement—and there will be false starts and reversals. Most of the career negotiations recounted to us by senior executives, managers, and other professionals lasted weeks or months. They started with preliminary conversations that gradually evolved, particularly as new information or the entrance of new players influenced the way various parties perceived their interests and the alternatives to agreement.

To maximize your odds of success, set targets for yourself that are specific and realistic—and that help hold you accountable to follow through with your plan amid pressing distractions and demands. Too often, negotiations fizzle or never get off the ground because larger goals become buried by everyday work.

One senior executive we interviewed told us, "You have a book to write of your life. Don't let anyone else write your chapters." We second that, but we also urge you to remember that great careers are not authored alone. Your narrative will be cowritten with work and life partners, and negotiation is at the heart of finding mutually gratifying ways for that story to unfold.

Originally published in January–February 2021. Reprint R2101E

Leading Through Anxiety

by Morra Aarons-Mele

THE CEO of a startup is sitting in the office space she recently leased for her fast-growing company. It's rush hour, but the streets outside are quiet, and so are the 600 empty cubicles outside her office door. Just yesterday her leadership team made the tough but crucial decision to send everyone home to work for the foreseeable future. In 30 minutes she needs to lead a videoconference to reassure her employees. But she's despondent, anxious, and just plain scared.

Versions of this scene have been playing out across the world over the past few months as Covid-19 cases rise and economies shut down. Founders, executives, managers, and employees have seen how fragile everything they've built has become—almost overnight. One evening back in March, my husband said to me, "I'm so scared, but I can't let all the people who depend on me see that." He had been on hours of Zoom calls, trying to convince his staff and colleagues that they would get through the crisis. He was supposed to be the face of calm, but he was terrified.

How can you lead with authority and strength when you feel anxious? How can you inspire and motivate others when your mind and heart are racing? And if you hide the fear in an attempt to be leader-like, where does it go?

Anxiety, of course, has a purpose. It protects us from harm. Psychologist Rollo May first wrote in 1977: "We are no longer prey to tigers and mastodons but to damage to our self-esteem, ostracism

The Big Idea: Managing in an Anxious World

"LEADING THROUGH ANXIETY" is the lead article of **HBR's The Big Idea: Managing in an Anxious World**. You can read the rest of the series at hbr.org/anxiety:

- "When Anxiety Becomes Unbearable," by Gretchen Gavett
- "5 Ways Leaders Accidentally Stress Out Their Employees," by Tomas Chamorro-Premuzic
- "How History's Great Leaders Managed Anxiety," by Alison Beard
- "Anxiety as a Public Health Issue," by Sandro Galea
- "How We Experience Anxiety Today," by Kelsey Gripenstraw

by our group, or the threat of losing out in the competitive struggle. The form of anxiety has changed, but the experience remains relatively the same." In other words, even though humans today aren't chased by predators, we are chased by uncertainty about the health of our loved ones, whether we'll have a job next week or next year, whether our company will go bankrupt—worries that provoke the same neurological and physical responses.

According to the Anxiety and Depression Association of America, "Stress is a response to a threat in a situation. Anxiety is a reaction to the stress." Anxiety is fear of what might happen in the future. Sometimes that fear is rational and sometimes not. And sometimes it's about something that will happen in three minutes (stepping onto a stage to make a presentation, for example) or in 30 years (having enough money to retire).

In the United States, anxiety is the most common mental illness, affecting more than 40 million adults each year. Data from the National Institute of Mental Health has indicated that about 30% of Americans experience clinical anxiety at some point in their lives. Globally, according to the Institute for Health Metrics and Evaluation, an estimated 284 million people had an anxiety disorder as of 2017, making it the most prevalent mental disorder worldwide. And

Idea in Brief

Anxiety isn't always counterproductive. It can prompt you to react quickly to threats, and in a crisis it can spur you to make your team more resourceful and productive. But unchecked, it zaps your energy and clouds your decisions. Anxiety is a powerful enemy; you need to disarm it. Morra Aarons-Mele offers advice on how you can inspire and encourage your team even when you're struggling yourself:

- First you must accept your anxiety and know what triggers it. Once you do that, you can begin managing it.

- Work to distinguish between the possible and the probable.

- Structure your time, take small, meaningful actions, and try techniques that reduce anxiety's physical symptoms.

- Set yourself up so that anxiety doesn't harm your ability to lead.

recent workplace data from Mind Share Partners, SAP, and Qualtrics suggests it's widespread on the job: Nearly 37% of workplace respondents reported symptoms of anxiety in the past year. These numbers will only increase in the wake of the pandemic.

The good news for those of us who have managed anxiety for a long time is that we were made for this moment. Data shows that anxious people process threats differently, using regions of the brain responsible for action. We react quickly in the face of danger. We may also be more comfortable with uncomfortable feelings. When channeled thoughtfully, anxiety can motivate us to make our teams more resourceful, productive, and creative. It can break down barriers and create new bonds.

So anxiety isn't useless. In an economic crisis, the anxiety that keeps us up at night may help us fathom a solution to keeping our businesses open. But left unchecked, anxiety distracts us, zaps our energy, and drives us to make poor decisions. Anxiety is a powerful enemy, so we must make it our partner.

Whether you have a diagnosed anxiety disorder or are having your first dance with this intense emotion, you can still be an effective leader. But I'll be blunt: If you don't look your anxiety in the face at some point, it will take you down. This isn't easy, but doing it will change your life and your ability to lead others for the better.

So today, in this especially anxious moment, let's begin. The first stage is learning to identify your anxiety: how it manifests itself and how it feels. The second stage is taking action to manage it both day-to-day and in challenging moments. The third stage entails making smart decisions and leading others in anxious times. Finally, the fourth stage involves building a support infrastructure to help you manage your anxiety over the long term.

Acknowledging and Accepting Your Emotions

A common coping mechanism for leaders is to push through stress, fatigue, and fear. But that's succeeding *in spite of* your emotions, when it's far better to thrive *because of* your emotions. You have to learn to accept your anxiety—even though this may seem uncomfortable or counterintuitive.

Label what you're feeling

Angela Neal-Barnett, an award-winning psychologist, expert on anxiety among African Americans, and author of *Soothe Your Nerves*, is a firm believer in being honest with yourself. When you name a feeling—by saying to yourself "I'm anxious"—you can begin to address it. You can learn how anxiety informs your behavior and your decisions and what causes it to surge, which will equip you to manage it.

No one has to hear you say it. This is for you. Take the time to wallow in your thoughts. Let yourself experience the discomfort of fear and anxiety. Play out worst-case scenarios in your head. Allow your imagination to go wild with catastrophe. Cry. Grieve. But don't turn away. As Alice Boyes, a former clinical psychologist and author of *The Anxiety Toolkit*, says: The more you try to control your anxiety, the more it fights back.

Decades of research on emotional intelligence have shown that people who understand their own feelings have higher job satisfaction, stronger job performance, and better relationships; are more innovative; and can synthesize diverse opinions and lessen conflict. And all those things make people better leaders.

If the word "anxiety" feels wrong to you, label it whatever you like. Call it "unease" or "temporary uncertainty" or even give it a silly name. I think of my own anxiety as a separate character who travels with me. She doesn't have a name or a face, but I know when she's present.

The leadership coach and CEO of Reboot, Jerry Colonna, says that the best way to deal with uncomfortable feelings is to welcome them in. Think of your thoughts and emotions as trains coming in and out of a station, he advises. Watch them arrive and depart without attachment. Imagine saying, "Hello, anxiety. See you later, fear." This technique actually will help you build distance from the negative feelings in your mind.

Sometimes it may be impossible to get rid of your anxiety, which can feel frustrating. Rebecca Harley, a psychologist at Massachusetts General Hospital and Harvard Medical School, emphasizes, "The goal is not to magically make things perfect. The goal is to learn to surf the waves of distress successfully. Give yourself credit even if things don't feel all the way better."

Play detective

Once you've labeled your anxiety, you can start pinpointing when it appears and why. Harley helped me learn to do this. When you feel anxious, take note of your physical reactions—what she calls the "early warning system" that anxiety might be taking over.

Your triggers might be small. You might notice a stomach flip and a spark of dread when you see someone's name pop up in your in-box. Or they might be bigger. When unemployment numbers skyrocket, you might feel nauseous and unable to focus even though you still have a job.

When an interaction or a situation sets you off, examine why. You might be hesitant to delve into issues from your childhood, but "unresolved business" from your past, as Colonna puts it, is very much present in—and relevant to—how you lead. He notes it can be a relief to truly understand how your old wounds inform your present behavior. When I realized that my near-constant worry about going broke stemmed more from my childhood than from my current financial situation, I was finally able to proactively manage my money, after years of avoiding it and piling up debt. I broke a damaging pattern.

It's also good to understand how you react when triggered. I call these anxiety "tells." Social worker and therapist Carolyn Glass suggests asking yourself, "How did I respond to that anxiety in that moment? And were those behaviors helpful or not? Did those behaviors fuel or alleviate my anxiety?" Glass says that writing down your fears will help you examine them. Keeping a journal of your anxiety—when it happens, what triggers it, and how you reacted—is a great way to develop self-awareness. Your tells may not always be negative behaviors, though; for instance, many of us find ourselves connecting with friends and family more during stressful times. When I'm very anxious, I cook and freeze meals!

Many successful leaders react to anxiety by working harder, holding themselves and others to an impossibly high standard, or trying to control things that are beyond their power. For them, it's hard to imagine *not* fussing over every project and detail in their work lives, not taking responsibility for everything or always giving their all. "People respond to anxiety by trying to be more perfect and more in control," Boyes says. "They not only have a Plan B but Plans C, D, and E." In many societies those behaviors are rewarded. We think of it as a "good work ethic," but often perfectionism and overwork only cause further anxiety—in yourself and others.

Imagine a CEO who is terrified by the economic news surrounding Covid-19. He jumps into the problem in the way that's worked for him in the past: making detailed projections on all aspects of the business. He buries himself in these charts while constantly consuming news about the crisis. Some of his team might wonder what he's up to or feel unsettled by his visible yet unspoken panic. Are the charts he furiously creates accurate? Who knows?! But the deep dive into worst-case scenario planning gives him the illusion of control.

Your tells may also be physical. Anxiety can manifest itself as tightness in the chest, shallow breathing, clenched jaw muscles, frozen shoulders, gastrointestinal symptoms, skin breakouts, appetite changes, and radical shifts in energy. When I recently had a panic attack, for example, I was convinced it was heart failure—even though I'd had panic attacks before.

To help you identify the ways anxiety may be physically affecting you, try this two-part exercise:

First, sit upright in a chair. Put your feet flat on the floor, and your hands on your lap. Keep your chin neutral. Note which part of the body you can immediately feel. Then, with your eyes closed, scan through the following:

- Your head

- Your jaw

- Your neck cords

- Your shoulders

- Your wrists and forearms

- Your chest

- Your upper back

- Your lower back

- Your stomach

- Your hips

- Your hamstrings and rear

- Your calves, ankles, and feet

Note which ones feel tight, and to gain some relief, breathe into the areas of tightness or pain.

You can also pay attention to what's happening with your body at different points during the workday, when specific events occur, or when you make certain decisions:

- How do you feel at 9 a.m., noon, and 3 and 6 p.m.? Does your body change over the course of the day?

- If you get stressed, does a particular part of your body react?

- How often do you rely on a drink, drug, muscle relaxant, or over-the-counter pain relief over the week?

- Does your body feel different after you exercise? Do your shoulders feel lighter?

- How does your body feel on the weekend or when you're doing something you enjoy?

Sort out the probable from the possible

Once you understand your triggers and tells, you can start developing a new relationship with your anxiety.

Remember, some anxiety is rational and helpful. In an economic downturn it makes sense for a leader to feel anxious. You might have to lay people off. Your business might fail. But you might find that you get stuck in a negative thought loop that prevents you from moving forward; you start obsessing. Boyes points out that some leaders get so focused on the worst-case scenario and overwhelmed by scary possibilities that they become frozen.

So how do you avoid being stuck? Here I turn to advice from Colonna: "Differentiate what's possible from what's probable. It is *possible* that everyone I love will die of a pandemic and I will lose everything I hold dear. But it's not *probable* that everything that we love and hold dear will disappear." Try to distinguish your worst fears from what is likely to happen. This will help calm you and give you space to move forward. So when a catastrophic thought comes into your head, such as "My partner and I are both going to lose our jobs" or "I'm definitely going to get sick," remember that you're an unreliable narrator when you're anxious. Check in with someone else you trust and ask for that person's help in telling what is likely to unfold from what is a long shot.

Back in early March, when the stock market first slumped and people's fears about Covid-19 spiked, one of my biggest clients canceled work with my small business. I quickly convinced myself that our company was doomed, that it would be only a matter of months before we had to close up shop. "We'll never survive this," I kept telling myself. But then I consulted my business partner—a more reliable narrator than I—and she suggested we readjust our forecast, which we did. Now we're projecting that we'll lose half our revenue for the year. This is probable and upsetting, but it's far different from going out of business completely.

Focusing on what's probable also takes flexibility—the future won't be what you thought, and that hurts. When my preschooler really wants to keep coloring, but it's time for dinner, I ask her, "Please be flexible. You can color later, I promise." I'm now trying to do what I've taught my kids for years: to handle the disappointment of things not going the way I expected or wanted. These disappointments are real, and sometimes the changes are grave. Acknowledge the grief and anger you feel (at least to yourself) and then make adjustments, identifying the aspects of your vision that may still work, and focus on what's probable.

Taking Action to Manage Your Anxiety

Once you make your way through these three steps, you can start to manage your anxiety daily in ways that allow you to grow as a leader and be more resourceful and productive.

The following tactics can help ground you.

Control what you can

Many faith traditions teach us to accept what we cannot control, without preoccupation or panic. But in the middle of an anxiety attack at work, you probably don't have time for philosophy. So here's what to do when things feel completely off the rails.

Structure your time. A solid body of research shows that improved "time management disposition"—meaning your attitude toward how you organize and value your time—has a positive impact on mental health. And it's especially crucial when you're gripped by anxiety.

First thing in the morning, create a to-do list and a detailed schedule for your day. I like to do it while having my coffee. You might use 30-minute increments to spell out when you'll shower, take a lunch break, make a phone call, or tackle that report that needs to get done. This is what many experts call "timeboxing." While you're at it, try to avoid what cognitive behavioral therapy terms "cognitive distortions." These are the catastrophic thoughts, self-judgments, and all-or-nothing ideas that often accompany anxiety.

Be careful not to overschedule or overestimate your productivity; instead focus on the critical work and leave time to take care of yourself.

Take small, meaningful actions. During the first few weeks of the coronavirus shutdown, traffic dropped drastically where I live. The local department of public works took that time to repaint all the crosswalks. For a week, roads were halfway blocked off as DPW crews painted. It wasn't a big deal because our normally bustling town was quiet. And each time I slowed down to drive past one of the crews, I smiled because it struck me: This is their small, meaningful action.

When you feel anxious, an immediate task can easily become overwhelming. Take running a cash flow analysis for your business. When you open up the accounting software, your mind might go to a dark place, and all of a sudden a month's worth of figures have spiraled into the business tanking and your losing your home. To break that mental spiral, take a small, meaningful action. If running a cash flow projection terrifies you, organize some receipts or clean up some file folders until the panic subsides.

In general, focus on the near term whenever you can. You may not be able to tell your employees what will happen next year—or even three months from now. You can't promise everything will be OK. But you *can* help your people be safe this week. Focus on that, and then deal with the big questions when you feel calmer or when you can get input from trusted colleagues. Sometimes you have to turn off the future for a little while and just manage through the present.

Develop techniques for situations you can't control

Of course, it's not always possible to turn off the future. What if your board needs those cash flow projections in the next 30 minutes and you're in a downward spiral? Here you'll want to have tools that help you calm down quickly so that you can get your job done.

Find a mindfulness technique that eases your acute anxiety
Neurologist Victor Frankl famously said, "Between stimulus and response there is a space. In that space is our power to choose our response. In our response lies our growth and our freedom." This is mindfulness in a nutshell. Even if you are high on anxiety and short on time, you can claim the space in between.

There are lots of ways to do this; the key is to find what's most effective for you. One option is to focus on your breathing. Belly breaths are a classic technique. Others prefer what's called "the 4-7-8 method." Either is simple to memorize and subtle enough to do at your desk. When you deliberately slow your breath, it sends a message to your brain to calm down, and your brain then sends the message to your body so that many of the physical symptoms of anxiety—such as increased heart rate and higher blood pressure—decrease.

You can also shift your attention. Glass says this technique is "great for someone who doesn't want to meditate but gets maladaptively anxious and cannot focus on anything else." Focus first on your anxiety, and then slowly turn your attention to something tangible, something you hold in your hand, like a book. By concentrating on an object in the present moment, you can turn the volume of your worry down until it's background noise.

If I'm full of anxious energy and unable to sit still, or if quiet breathing exercises don't work, I like to loudly blast a favorite song and dance for five minutes. Some people like to sing instead. Experiment with what works for you and then keep that tactic in your back pocket for when you need it.

Compartmentalize or postpone your worry. Sometimes I talk out loud to my anxiety, saying, "Sorry, I'm going to deal with you after I finish my work." You may want to write the worry down and save it for a specific time—maybe later that day or your next session with your therapist.

In times of crisis you may actually find that things that worried you in the past fade into the background. The urgency of what's happening in the moment takes over. To stop your anxiety from sneaking into the foreground, you might tell it, "You can stay where you are. I'm part of the solution here, and I need to get this task done."

Make a connection. Connecting with others can break the negative thought loop that often accompanies anxiety. Instead of focusing on yourself, you turn your attention outward. When I asked my friend and colleague Cheryl Contee, the CEO and cofounder of the digital agency Do Big Things, how she was staying motivated during the crisis, she said that she was trying to "be a good neighbor," something she learned from her grandfather, William G. Contee, who has a park dedicated to him in his Baltimore neighborhood. "Being a good neighbor is surprisingly simple—it's just about connecting on the human level," she told me. "Do you say hello to your neighbors? Have you asked how they're doing or if they need anything?"

Contee also connects digitally with people in her field, who support one another and contribute to causes they care about. At her company she and her colleagues are leaning into talking about their feelings and families, doing a lot of checking about how to balance homeschooling with work. "We're all veteran virtual knowledge workers, but having kids around and being responsible for their education is a new challenge we're facing together," she said.

In your own life, think about performing a quick, generous act. You might check in on a former colleague via text message. Or ask a family member how you might help. When I'm feeling anxious, I sometimes go to LinkedIn and "like" articles written by my colleagues or write up an endorsement of their work. This gets me out of my head and focused on something more positive.

Finally, if anxiety is persistent and hampering your days, you might consider consulting a therapist or mental health professional. Talking to someone trained in helping others manage anxiety may give you additional coping mechanisms to address debilitating symptoms.

Limiting Anxiety's Impact on Your Leadership

Once you have a better sense of how you experience anxiety and how you can manage it daily, it's time to turn to how it affects your leadership and management abilities.

Make good decisions

Anxiety can impair our judgment. It can cause us to focus on the wrong things, distort the facts, or rush to conclusions. Ideally, we could postpone critical decisions until we're in a better frame of mind, but that's not always possible.

In anxious times it's important to proactively set yourself up to make good choices. Much as you do when separating the possible from the probable, start by acknowledging that your emotions can make you an unreliable narrator and that you will likely be prone to negative thoughts. Let's say you're prepping for a speech and the last time you spoke to a group of a similar size, you felt that you bombed. You may even have a long-held belief that you're a terrible public speaker because a middle school recitation drew snickers. Ask yourself: Are you being objective? If you're not sure, check whether your memory is correct, perhaps by asking a colleague who was in the room for feedback.

Of course, you need to ask the right people. Boyes suggests you find a trusted adviser with a decision-making style that differs from your own. If you're impulsive, consult someone who is methodical and conservative, for example.

Ultimately, every leader should develop a team of "real talk" peers: people who will provide their unvarnished opinions. You can fill this role for others, too. You can still offer them clarity and insight even if you're an unreliable narrator of your own experience.

Practice healthy communication

One of the most dangerous aspects of anxiety is that it's contagious, and leaders set the tone. Daniel Goleman, the renowned psychologist and author of *Emotional Intelligence*, calls this "neural Wi-Fi," in which humans pick up on others' unspoken feelings.

If you're not admitting that you're anxious but instead emitting irritability or distraction, you're not doing your staff any favors. But how can you be honest with your people in a way that doesn't strike fear in them? What degree of emotion is appropriate to express?

Ultimately, how much you disclose is a personal decision. As an owner of a business and the host of a podcast about anxiety and mental health, I tend to be an open book. But I know that most leaders don't share their demons. Few feel comfortable starting a staff meeting with "Wow, I'm anxious today."

But self-aware leaders know when it's appropriate to be vulnerable. And here's the thing: Your staff needs you to be transparent and honest about anxiety and mental health, especially when the future of your company and their livelihoods are uncertain.

Amelia Ransom, the senior director of engagement and diversity at Avalara, says that she wants her leaders to admit when they're not doing OK, because it affirms her experience. "It makes me feel normal if someone I respect and trust admits they aren't all right. I think, 'Thank you for being human,' and I want to follow that person." Ransom recounts a powerful moment when a senior executive in her company brought the staff together on a videoconference and said, "I can't tell you, 'You got this.' What I can do is hold space for us to be together right now, to talk and figure some things out."

Admitting "I'm anxious today" or "I didn't sleep well" lets everyone else in the room breathe a little easier. ("Phew, it's not my fault he is so tense.") And remember, you don't have to share details; just share the state you're in.

The social psychologist Amy Cuddy tells us we need leaders who exhibit both warmth and strength. "Most leaders today tend to emphasize their strength, competence, and credentials in the workplace, but that is exactly the wrong approach," she writes. "Leaders who project strength before establishing trust run the risk of eliciting fear, and along with it a host of dysfunctional behaviors." Nothing establishes trust more effectively than the emotional connection fostered through empathy and shared humanity. This is why being open about your own anxiety can be so powerful. It builds trust when you can ask teammates, "How are you?" and they don't feel as if they have to lie or put on a happy face, because they know you feel the strain, too.

This doesn't mean that you fall into a puddle of tears during a videoconference, of course, or visibly lose control. And while your workers might want to know that you're closely monitoring cash flow to make sure bills get paid, they don't need to know that your anxiety is deeply rooted in your parents' money troubles during your childhood. It's possible to model taking care of your mental health without making people lose confidence in your competence.

Imagine you're in an anxiety spiral from reading news about Covid-19, but you need to lead a staff meeting in 10 minutes. You could open the meeting by saying, "Obviously, the news is getting more upsetting by the minute, but I want us to put that aside for the next half hour while we go through this call." Or you could be even more vulnerable and share that you're working to contain your scary thoughts by giving yourself what Glass calls a "worry hour," when you allow yourself to indulge your biggest concerns before putting them away again and forging on.

If you want to encourage people to share but don't want the conversation to slip into an anxiety fest, you can use a red-yellow-green exercise. Team members individually indicate where their moods are that day with one of the three colors, and they can expand on why if they wish. This allows people to share if they feel comfortable doing so and gives you useful information about the emotions of the group. You can then adjust your communication style and messaging accordingly.

And remember, while being positive is important to prevent emotional contagion, you don't want to give anyone false hope. If you get tough questions like "Is my job safe?" or "Will we be in business in six months?" it's not your job to divine the future. No one has a crystal ball, and so you can say what you know to be true in this moment and affirm the importance of working together and focusing on what each person can control.

Building a Support System

The final step in leading through anxiety is making sure you have ongoing support. This means not only surrounding yourself with the right people but also developing routines that help you deal with bouts of anxiety and lay the groundwork for maintaining your mental health.

Schedule, structure, and scenario plan

When you have anxiety, you need to be intentional about what your days look like, as I discussed earlier. The methods are basic: making lists, prioritizing, and breaking work into manageable chunks. Chop tasks that make you extremely anxious into bearable pieces. I learned this trick from my own psychiatrist, Carol Birnbaum.

Also use the detective work you did about your triggers to prepare for situations or events you know will cause you anxiety. If public speaking stresses you out, make sure you leave plenty of time to rehearse presentations. If you're afraid of flying, mentally rehearse a business trip from "I'm going to pack" to "I'm going to order a cab and call my friend while I'm on my way to the airport" to "I'll buy M&M's when I get there because they make me happy." And finally, once on the plane: "I'm going to take a Xanax, do a calming meditation, and survive."

I get anxious when I'm working far from home and haven't heard from my nanny or husband. I worry something bad has happened and get distracted from what I'm supposed to be doing. To counter this I ask my husband or the babysitter to text me with an update every three hours. That way I don't pester them when they might be driving with the kids in the car, for example. And knowing that they will keep me updated allows me to sink into my work.

Know who your "safe team" is

Since you want to spare your employees the messy details of your anxiety, you need a place for those emotions to go. Make sure you have a "safe team" of people to whom you can confess scary thoughts. They can include a therapist, a coach, a mentor, a spouse or partner, and friends. It could be an intimate group of fellow leaders, online or off-line, who commit to sharing in confidence and making space for one another's difficult emotions.

Practice self-care

I don't need to belabor this point. You know what self-care means for you, whether it's sleep, exercise, hobbies, massage, spending time alone, or being with people you love. The point is, take it seriously, as if your doctor had written you a prescription for it. It's neither frivolous nor optional for you as a leader. And aspects of it you feel comfortable sharing can benefit your team: When you model good practices, others feel permission to take care of themselves, too. This could be as simple as letting people know that you don't take your phone upstairs when you head to bed, that you're taking an hour during the workday to exercise, or that you're limiting exposure to news or Twitter.

Putting in place the support infrastructure to manage your anxiety will help you ride out setbacks and tough times. It's a strategy for long-term success and sustainability as a leader. It means you'll have better workdays, both when things are status quo and during transitions and tough times.

Ultimately, anxiety comes with the job of being a leader. The process of managing it can make you stronger, more empathetic, and more effective. It just might be bumpy along the way. So remember to treat yourself with compassion. Recognize that you're doing the best you can, that your emotions are normal, and that the healthiest thing you can do is to allow yourself to experience them.

Far too many of us think it's taboo to talk about mental health at work. I know many leaders who don't feel as if they can walk into a staff meeting and say, "I'm anxious today."

Why not? And why not now? These are not normal times, and acknowledging a universal emotion can help people understand that what they're feeling is OK.

We're in desperate need of better models of leadership, especially when society tells us that anxiety and depression are weaknesses.

The data bears this out: A 2019 Mind Share Partners report found that 86% of U.S. job seekers thought it was important for an employer's culture to support mental health, but only 37% of employees saw their company leaders as advocates for mental health at work.

This time of crisis—in which those of us with a history of anxiety may be experiencing it acutely while others may be feeling it intensely for the first time—is an opportunity to change that perception.

You can play a role in telling a different story.

When Anxiety Becomes Unbearable

by Gretchen Gavett

Maybe you've been anxious all your life. Maybe the Covid-19 pandemic has taken it to an unprecedented level. Or maybe you don't suffer from anxiety but work with people who do.

Even if you're used to managing it on a day-to-day basis, it's not always clear when anxiety is cause for concern. So I asked **Dr. Ellen Hendriksen,** a clinical psychologist and the author of *How to Be Yourself: Quiet Your Inner Critic and Rise Above Social Anxiety*, about the warning signs that someone is really struggling.

Dr. Hendriksen offered advice on addressing heightened anxiety with humanity and compassion and, when the person struggling is a work colleague, discussing it without overstepping. Our conversation, which took place over email, has been edited for clarity.

HBR: *What are the signs that your anxiety is reaching an unsustainable level?*

Hendriksen: We know anxiety has escaped its confines and is running wild when it surpasses the thresholds of distress or impairment. *Distress* means intense stress is overwhelming your usual ways of coping. Maybe you've always been able to manage your anxiety with yoga, a sense of humor, or some healthy perspective, but now nothing seems to keep the lid on. *Impairment* means the anxiety is getting in the way of living your life. For instance, you can't focus, so you're behind on your work, are losing sleep, or are so preoccupied that you can't be present with your kids or partner.

What should you look out for in your boss, colleagues, or employees?

Problematic anxiety is mostly internal and therefore is hard to spot. However, clues include unmanageable worry or irritability, inability to focus or concentrate, and physical restlessness (pacing, being on edge). In conversation, or on a Zoom call, you can often sense the person has tunnel vision—they might be hyperfocused on a worry, keep coming back to a topic, or refuse to consider others' points of view.

In addition, problematic anxiety often leads to under-control or overcontrol. People who under-control can be passive or all over the place. Their actions can be scattered, inefficient, and unhelpful—you might find yourself thinking, "What are they *doing*?" They either follow every impulse or give up altogether, bending as the wind blows.

Overcontrol can take the form of micromanagement, rigidity, hypervigilance for potential threats, refusing to try new approaches or adapt, or insisting that there is a right way to do things. There are the folks who, during a time of high anxiety, throw themselves into work or anything else they can control, from financial planning to making a spreadsheet of their canned goods.

But remember: Overcontrol is a problem only when it causes distress or impairment to the anxious person or to those around them. Focusing on work is fine if it gets someone's mind off the crisis, but if work becomes their *only* focus, and especially if their health or relationships suffer as a result, they have crossed the line into unhealthy overcontrol. Keep this in mind for yourself as well.

Pretty much everyone has a relatively high level of anxiety at the moment. How can you differentiate that from something more troubling?

It is important that someone's response isn't disproportionate to the threat. Before Covid-19, it would have been over the top to wear gloves and a mask while grocery shopping. These days everything has changed. A higher-than-normal level of anxiety is expected and appropriate. But the disproportion rule still applies: For example, refusing to go to the emergency room if your appendix bursts, or hitting the grocery store in full scuba gear, is still generally considered to be over the line.

Give everyone plenty of slack, understanding, and validation. Also, when someone seems especially anxious, keep in mind that you may not know the full context. Maybe their sister is a nurse on the front lines in New York. Maybe their spouse was laid off and they're worried about paying the mortgage. Maybe they have an underlying condition that puts them in a high-risk group. Their anxiety may not be disproportionate at all.

What are some things you shouldn't say to a colleague who seems anxious? And what can you do that might actually help?

Don't try to offer quick fixes: "Have you tried yoga?" or "I hear lavender essential oil can work wonders." Advice like that, while well-intentioned, comes across as invalidating—"Oh, is that all I have to do? Silly me!" Worse, offering advice creates an expert/amateur dynamic, rather than a relationship of equals.

Likewise, dismissals like "Calm down," "There's nothing to be afraid of," or "Just don't worry about it" feel invalidating and unsupportive.

Many people feel uneasy about offering help to a colleague they're not close to. But no matter the depth of your relationship, you can always validate their experience ("It totally makes sense that we're all stressed right now" or "Trust me, nobody is doing their best work these days") or make a workplace-appropriate disclosure of your own ("It's been a real challenge to juggle everything" or "The worst part for me is not knowing how or when all this will end").

Some worries are expressed as "what ifs"—"What if I get quarantined and can't work?" or "What if my elderly parents get sick?" Know that the "what if" is rhetorical, but go ahead and inquire about an answer: "That's a scary thought. What *would* you do?" Anxiety is driven by uncertainty, and generating a plan creates certainty, which in turn can reduce anxiety. Supporting your colleague as they think through a plan of action (without proffering advice—refrain from

"I'll tell you what worked for my brother") can be helpful without invalidating their fears.

What should you do if you, a colleague, or an employee has a panic attack?

Panic attacks feel awful. It sounds silly, but remind yourself (or your colleague) that it's a panic attack. It's easy to get caught up in the feeling that you might be dying, are having a heart attack, or have finally snapped and lost it. But remember, it's a panic attack, and panic attacks always end. What goes up must come down.

Next, if you or your colleague has prescribed medication for panic, this is the time to take it.

If you're at home and have a panic attack, a nonmedication response is to fill a sink or a big bowl with cold water, add ice cubes if you can, and dunk your face in. Hold your breath and keep your face immersed for 30 seconds. This triggers the *diving reflex,* which is an evolutionary response that shuts down all nonessential body functions—including strong emotion—during a fall into cold water. It kicks in the parasympathetic nervous system and calms you down. Alternatives include taking a cold shower or putting an ice pack over your eyes and holding your breath for 30 seconds.

If you're trying to help a colleague, don't chatter anxiously at them or pepper them with questions. Stay as calm as you can and ask them to breathe deeply and—most important—slowly! Rapid breathing can mimic hyperventilation and make a panic attack feel worse. Ask them to inhale for a count of six and exhale for a count of 10. This takes advantage of a natural physiological phenomenon called *respiratory sinus arrhythmia,* which means your heart beats faster on an inhale and slower on an exhale. If you exhale for longer than you inhale, over time your heart rate will slow, which in turn will calm your other body systems.

What if someone's workplace performance suffers over time because of continued anxiety? How should managers and employers respond?

Managers can't and shouldn't ask about private health information. But they can address specific tasks or behaviors. If deadlines are being missed or projects are falling perilously behind, you can start a conversation. Use the same tone you would in asking about a physical illness or injury—be caring and open. Tiptoeing makes things awkward and can backfire. Say: "I wanted to check in given the last few deadlines. I know this crisis has been a big challenge for everyone. You don't have to navigate this all by yourself. Let's talk about how we can support you." Or say: "I want to acknowledge that things have been really stressful and uncertain lately. It's not your style to let things fall behind, so I wanted to check in. You're such a vital and extraordinary part of this team; let's make sure you have what you need."

This is a great time for both you and your employees to take advantage of any mental health benefits your workplace offers, like an employee assistance or behavioral health program. During this crisis, many therapists are offering telehealth sessions through health care–compliant platforms. And even though privacy can be hard to come by with kids and partners within earshot, enterprising folks have taken their laptops out to their parked cars for online therapy sessions, or talked to their therapists on the phone in our nearly empty streets.

What happens now that many of us are working from home? How can you stay on the pulse of your employees' anxiety virtually, without being too invasive or violating anyone's privacy?

It's OK to be more direct than usual given the circumstances. Working remotely, it's harder to pick up on the same signs you would see in person.

Be transparent—acknowledge that it's a difficult time for everyone and you want to check in. Ask how they're doing and how you can help. If they say, "I'm fine," don't respond with "Great!" and mentally check off the box. Instead, respond with a spirit of flexibility and openness: "If that changes, let me know" or "I'm so glad—let's keep checking in as the weeks go by." Everything that makes you a good human—sincerity, flexibility, caring about your colleagues—will make you a good manager in this unprecedented time.

5 Ways Leaders Accidentally Stress Out Their Employees

by Tomas Chamorro-Premuzic

Decades of scientific research show that stress and anxiety are prevalent problems at work, contributing to deficits in employee morale, well-being, and productivity. While anxiety is caused by a range of factors, including issues unrelated to people's jobs, one common and pervasive cause *is* something specific to the workplace: incompetent leadership.

Managers and leaders have a direct effect on their employees' stress and anxiety levels. What they say, feel, and do hugely influences their team's physical and emotional well-being. And the more senior leaders are, the more people they are likely to influence—positively and negatively.

But sadly, far too few leaders are aware that they have this power. And many are overconfident in their leadership skills, creating a gap between their perceived and actual levels of competence. This explains why even well-meaning bosses may inadvertently contribute to high anxiety levels in their employees and have a limited capacity to correct and improve their behavior: If you think you are leading effectively, what is the point of changing?

It is for this reason that leaders must pay a great deal of attention to how they act and communicate. The importance of this is exacerbated during times of increased uncertainty, as we often look to leaders to guide us in the face of fear, to provide us with clarity and direction, and, most of all, to give us reasons to remain hopeful and optimistic.

If you are a manager or a leader, it is useful to internalize some key psychological lessons about how your behavior—what you say, do, feel, and express—impacts your team, especially when you are not aware of it. In particular, there are five behavioral patterns that most often increase people's anxiety level. If you can spot them, you can learn how to change them in order to become a more effective leader.

1. The use of negative language

Too often we focus on nonverbal communication as a signal for conveying emotions—how we move our hands or which facial expressions we make—when in reality, the words we say are more likely to convey how we feel and what we think. As the growing field of algorithmic text mining and natural language processing shows, there is a systematic and robust connection between the type and frequency of words we choose to express ourselves and our moods and temperaments.

This means that even when you think you're discussing your business strategy dispassionately, the way you talk about it and the language you choose will convey your emotional and mental state to others—irrespective of your intentions. Leaders in particular can expect the emotional impact of their words to be even stronger when they are written. People tend to reread important messages, internalizing their affective content.

Research has shown that to avoid accidentally triggering anxiety through language, best practice is to refrain from using *negative words* (for example, *horrific, shocking,* and *dangerous,* as well as euphemisms such as *challenging, problematic,* and *undesirable*). In fact, the only criterion for determining whether a word is negative is whether it increases the listener's negative affect—in other words, that it might elevate their levels of anxiety, worry, and concern. Even if two leaders are in the same situation and describing the same state of affairs, they will have a different effect on the public if they talk about "hope," "improvements," or "light at the end of the tunnel" as opposed to "death toll," "mortality rate," or "depression."

2. Unusual or erratic actions

We often celebrate spontaneity and unpredictability as critical ingredients of creativity, as if they were integral components of a free spirit. In reality, however, most people want to eliminate as much uncertainty and unpredictability from their lives as they can, as both tend to trigger anxiety.

The Covid-19 pandemic makes this clear. We are shocked not only by the virus's devasting effects on our lives but also by our inability to predict what will happen. There is not much certainty leaders can provide when they are equally unable to predict the future. But they can, at the very least, avoid being an additional stress agent by acting in consistent and predictable ways.

If you are a boss, don't introduce an unnecessary layer of complexity to your employees' lives by making them guess what you will do next. Be reliable, predictable, and even boring if necessary. You may be the only predictable factor your employees can count on in a time of great uncertainty.

In simple terms, this means providing a clear structure to your meetings and communications, sharing expectations up front, avoiding last-minute changes and cancellations, and, wherever possible, continuing with the same routine you had before the crisis or big change.

3. Emotional volatility

Excitable bosses are like a roller coaster—they may be fun for sensation seekers, but they are stressful for almost everyone else. The last thing your employees want during difficult times is to see emotional volatility in their leaders. It is a bit like provoking someone into an emotional discussion when they've had a really bad day—it is not going to end well.

This may be easier said than done, but being a leader requires a certain level of competence for dealing with pressure. Especially in a crisis, remember that your own stress will only amplify other people's stress. The main implication here is that you should work very hard to manage your impressions, contain your emotions, and put on your best poker face in front of your employees.

What might this look like? In general—and this goes back to the second point—your team is looking to you for stability and guidance amid the chaos. If you are typically calm and stable, try to remain so as much as possible. Even if it may be normal to display some degree of emotional volatility during a crisis, the fewer changes your team perceives from your typical patterns of behavior, the less stressed they will be. If your natural style is volatile and reactive, however, you may be better off projecting an aura of calmness and composure, as if you had just taken up meditation. This shift may feel extreme to you personally, but over time it will help you better tame or filter your own anxiety. Once your team begins to notice the change, they may feel less on edge themselves, too.

Actions that have been found to mitigate emotional volatility include a regular practice of mindfulness, frequent exercise, better sleep quality, and internalizing feedback from others so that you realize when you may be derailing.

4. Excessive pessimism

We live in a world—especially in the West—that stigmatizes negativity and condemns pessimism as if it were a psychological problem. In fact, pessimism is underrated, as it helps leaders to detect and prevent potential threats, minimize risks, and avoid arrogant and overconfident decisions. That said, during stressful and anxious times leaders' pessimism is more likely to turn into a liability, demotivating others and pushing their already high anxiety to stressful levels.

This is why, even when you cannot find reasons to project optimism, you should still refrain from displaying outright pessimism. Even if your natural response is to feel pessimistic, projecting this onto others may further their anxiety. Being able to control it and project calmness and composure will strengthen your colleagues. Remember that leadership is not about you; it's a resource you provide to help others.

Further, because it's likely that your team expects a certain degree of optimism from you during uncertain times, they may already discount for this. If you say things will be great, they will believe you; but if you tell them things will be bad, they may interpret the situation as worse than it is.

5. Ignoring people's emotions

Perhaps the biggest mistake you can make during stressful times is ignoring your team's emotions. This error often occurs when a leader is hyperfocused on dealing with their *own* emotions. While you need to understand your own anxiety and get it under control, it is also critical to manage how others are perceiving your well-being. If they think you cannot manage yourself, they won't trust you to manage them. The key here is empathy: You will only succeed if you are focused on the people around you, not on yourself.

In the past two decades, a great deal of research has highlighted the key role that emotional intelligence (EQ) plays in developing empathy. More specifically, we have learned that leaders with a high EQ are better at understanding and influencing other people's emotions, as well as controlling their own. Some leaders are naturally better at this than others. Unfortunately, no one will suddenly wake up with a higher EQ overnight. But they *can* work on their willingness to understand other people.

A critical starting point is remembering that during difficult times it is more important to monitor people's affect, mood, and stress rather than check on their work performance, productivity, or task management. Simple ways to achieve this are to have more one-on-one meetings with team members, increase the frequency of your communication, ask open-ended questions that invite people to engage, and show empathy whenever possible. As the great Dale Carnegie put it, "When dealing with people, remember you are not dealing with creatures of logic, but creatures of emotion."

In short, you will be less likely to increase anxiety in others if you make a commitment to thinking more deeply about how your actions impact them. As a leader, you are an amplifier of people's emotions. If you do things right, you can bring out the best in people even in the worst of times. If you do things wrong, you will lower morale and performance even when things are fine.

Originally published in May 2020. Reprint H05LK7

When Machine Learning Goes Off the Rails

by Boris Babic, I. Glenn Cohen, Theodoros Evgeniou, and Sara Gerke

WHAT HAPPENS WHEN machine learning—computer programs that absorb new information and then change how they make decisions— leads to investment losses, biased hiring or lending, or car accidents? Should businesses allow their smart products and services to autonomously evolve, or should they "lock" their algorithms and periodically update them? If firms choose to do the latter, when and how often should those updates happen? And how should companies evaluate and mitigate the risks posed by those and other choices?

Across the business world, as machine-learning-based artificial intelligence permeates more and more offerings and processes, executives and boards must be prepared to answer such questions. In this article, which draws on our work in health care law, ethics, regulation, and machine learning, we introduce key concepts for understanding and managing the potential downside of this advanced technology.

What Makes Machine Learning Risky

The big difference between machine learning and the digital technologies that preceded it is the ability to independently make increasingly complex decisions—such as which financial products to trade, how vehicles react to obstacles, and whether a patient has a disease—and continuously adapt in response to new data. But these algorithms don't always work smoothly. They don't always make ethical or accurate choices. There are three fundamental reasons for this.

One is simply that the algorithms typically rely on the *probability* that someone will, say, default on a loan or have a disease. Because they make so many predictions, it's likely that *some* will be wrong, just because there's always a chance that they'll be off. The likelihood of errors depends on a lot of factors, including the amount and quality of the data used to train the algorithms, the specific type of machine-learning method chosen (for example, deep learning, which uses complex mathematical models, versus classification trees that rely on decision rules), and whether the system uses only *explainable algorithms* (meaning humans can describe how they arrived at their decisions), which may not allow it to maximize accuracy.

Second, the environment in which machine learning operates may itself evolve or differ from what the algorithms were developed to face. While this can happen in many ways, two of the most frequent are *concept drift* and *covariate shift*.

With the former the relationship between the inputs the system uses and its outputs isn't stable over time or may be misspecified. Consider a machine-learning algorithm for stock trading. If it has been trained using data only from a period of low market volatility and high economic growth, it may not perform well when the economy enters a recession or experiences turmoil—say, during a crisis like the Covid-19 pandemic. As the market changes, the relationship between the inputs and outputs—for example, between how leveraged a company is and its stock returns—also may change. Similar misalignment may happen with credit-scoring models at different points in the business cycle.

In medicine, an example of concept drift is when a machine-learning-based diagnostic system that uses skin images as inputs in detecting skin cancers fails to make correct diagnoses because the relationship between, say, the color of someone's skin (which may

Idea in Brief

The Problem

Offerings that rely on machine learning are proliferating, raising all sorts of new risks for companies that develop and use them or supply data to train them. That's because such systems don't always make ethical or accurate choices.

The Causes

First, the systems often make decisions based on probabilities. Second, their environments may evolve in an unanticipated way. Third, their complexity makes it difficult to determine whether or why they made a mistake.

The Solutions

Executives must decide whether to let a system continuously evolve or introduce locked versions at intervals. In addition, they should test the offering appropriately before and after it is rolled out and monitor it constantly once it's on the market.

vary with race or sun exposure) and the diagnosis decision hasn't been adequately captured. Such information often is not even available in electronic health records used to train the machine-learning model.

Covariate shifts occur when the data fed into an algorithm during its use differs from the data that trained it. This can happen even if the patterns the algorithm learned are stable and there's no concept drift. For example, a medical device company may develop its machine-learning-based system using data from large urban hospitals. But once the device is out in the market, the medical data fed into the system by care providers in rural areas may not look like the development data. The urban hospitals might have a higher concentration of patients from certain sociodemographic groups who have underlying medical conditions not commonly seen in rural hospitals. Such disparities may be discovered only when the device makes more errors while out in the market than it did during testing. Given the diversity of markets and the pace at which they're changing, it's becoming increasingly challenging to foresee what will happen in the environment that systems operate in, and no amount of data can capture all the nuances that occur in the real world.

The third reason machine learning can make inaccurate decisions has to do with the complexity of the overall systems it's embedded in.

Consider a device used to diagnose a disease on the basis of images that doctors input—such as IDx-DR, which identifies eye disorders like diabetic retinopathy and macular edema and was the first autonomous machine-learning-based medical device authorized for use by the U.S. Food and Drug Administration. The quality of any diagnosis depends on how clear the images provided are, the specific algorithm used by the device, the data that algorithm was trained with, whether the doctor inputting the images received appropriate instruction, and so on. With so many parameters, it's difficult to assess whether and why such a device may have made a mistake, let alone be certain about its behavior.

But inaccurate decisions are not the only risks with machine learning. Let's look now at two other categories: agency risk and moral risk.

Agency Risk

The imperfections of machine learning raise another important challenge: risks stemming from things that aren't under the control of a specific business or user.

Ordinarily, it's possible to draw on reliable evidence to reconstruct the circumstances that led to an accident. As a result, when one occurs, executives can at least get helpful estimates of the extent of their company's potential liability. But because machine learning is typically embedded within a complex system, it will often be unclear what led to a breakdown—which party, or "agent" (for example, the algorithm developer, the system deployer, or a partner), was responsible for an error and whether there was an issue with the algorithm, with some data fed to it by the user, or with the data used to train it, which may have come from multiple third-party vendors. Environmental change and the probabilistic nature of machine learning make it even harder to attribute responsibility to a particular agent. In fact, accidents or unlawful decisions can occur even without negligence on anyone's part—as there is simply always the possibility of an inaccurate decision.

Executives need to know when their companies are likely to face liability under current law, which may itself also evolve. Consider the medical context. Courts have historically viewed doctors as the final decision-makers and have therefore been hesitant to apply product liability to medical software makers. However, this may change as more black-box or autonomous systems make diagnoses and recommendations without the involvement of (or with much weaker involvement by) physicians in clinics. What will happen, for example, if a machine-learning system recommends a nonstandard treatment for a patient (like a much higher drug dosage than usual) and regulation evolves in such a way that the doctor would most likely be held liable for any harm only if he or she did not follow the system's recommendation? Such regulatory changes may shift liability risks from doctors to the developers of the machine-learning-enabled medical devices, the data providers involved in developing the algorithms, or the companies involved in installing and deploying the algorithms.

Moral Risk

Products and services that make decisions autonomously will also need to resolve ethical dilemmas—a requirement that raises additional risks and regulatory and product development challenges. Scholars have now begun to frame these challenges as problems of *responsible algorithm design*. They include the puzzle of how to automate moral reasoning. Should Tesla, for example, program its cars to think in utilitarian cost-benefit terms or Kantian ones, where certain values cannot be traded off regardless of benefits? Even if the answer is utilitarian, quantification is extremely difficult: How should we program a car to value the lives of three elderly people against, say, the life of one middle-aged person? How should businesses balance trade-offs among, say, privacy, fairness, accuracy, and security? Can all those kinds of risks be avoided?

Moral risks also include biases related to demographic groups. For example, facial-recognition algorithms have a difficult time identifying people of color; skin-lesion-classification systems appear to have unequal accuracy across race; recidivism-prediction instruments give Blacks and Hispanics falsely high ratings, and credit-scoring systems give them unjustly low ones. With many widespread commercial uses, machine-learning systems may be deemed unfair to a certain group on some dimensions.

The problem is compounded by the multiple and possibly mutually incompatible ways to define fairness and encode it in algorithms. A lending algorithm can be calibrated—meaning that its decisions are independent of group identity after controlling for risk level—while still disproportionately denying loans to creditworthy minorities. As a result, a company can find itself in a "damned if you do, damned if you don't" situation. If it uses algorithms to decide who receives a loan, it may have difficulty avoiding charges that it's discriminating against some groups according to one of the definitions of fairness. Different cultures may also accept different definitions and ethical trade-offs—a problem for products with global markets. A February 2020 European Commission white paper on AI points to these challenges: It calls for the development of AI with "European values," but will such AI be easily exported to regions with different values?

Finally, all these problems can also be caused by model instability. This is a situation where inputs that are close to one another lead to decisions that are far apart. Unstable algorithms are likely to treat very similar people very differently—and possibly unfairly.

All these considerations, of course, don't mean that we should avoid machine learning altogether. Instead, executives need to embrace the opportunities it creates while making sure they properly address the risks.

To Lock or Not to Lock?

If leaders decide to employ machine learning, a key next question is: Should the company allow it to continuously evolve or instead introduce only tested and locked versions at intervals? Would the latter choice mitigate the risks just described?

This problem is familiar to the medical world. The FDA has so far typically approved only "software as a medical device" (software that can perform its medical functions without hardware) whose algorithms are locked. The reasoning: The agency has not wanted to permit the use of devices whose diagnostic procedures or treatment pathways keep changing in ways it doesn't understand. But as the FDA and other regulators are now realizing, locking the algorithms may be just as risky, because it doesn't necessarily remove the following dangers:

Inaccurate decisions

Locking doesn't alter the fact that machine-learning algorithms typically base decisions on estimated probabilities. Moreover, while the input of more data usually leads to better performance, it doesn't always, and the amount of improvement can vary; improvements in unlocked algorithms may be greater or smaller for different systems and with different volumes of data. Though it's difficult to understand how the accuracy (or inaccuracy) of decisions may change when an algorithm is unlocked, it's important to try.

Environmental changes

It also matters whether and how the environment in which the system makes decisions is evolving. For example, car autopilots operate in environments that are constantly altered by the behavior of other drivers. Pricing, credit scoring, and trading systems may face a shifting market regime whenever the business cycle enters a new phase. The challenge is ensuring that the machine-learning system and the environment coevolve in a way that lets the system make appropriate decisions.

Agency risks

Locking an algorithm doesn't eliminate the complexity of the system in which it's embedded. For example, errors caused by using inferior data from third-party vendors to train the algorithm or by differences in skills across users can still occur. Liability can still be challenging to assign across data providers, algorithm developers, deployers, and users.

Moral risks

A locked system may preserve imperfections or biases unknown to its creators. When analyzing mammograms for signs of breast cancer, a locked algorithm would be unable to learn from new subpopulations to which it is applied. Since average breast density can differ by race, this could lead to misdiagnoses if the system screens people from a demographic group that was underrepresented in the training data. Similarly, a credit-scoring algorithm trained on a socioeconomically segregated subset of the population can discriminate against certain borrowers in much the same way that the illegal practice of redlining does. We want algorithms to correct for such problems as soon as possible by updating themselves as they "observe" more data from subpopulations that may not have been well represented or even identified before. Conversely, devices whose machine-learning systems are not locked could harm one or more groups over time if they're evolving by using mostly data from a different group. What's more, identifying the point at which the device gets comparatively worse at treating one group can be hard.

A Tool Kit for Executives

So how should executives manage the existing and emerging risks of machine learning? Developing appropriate processes, increasing the savviness of management and the board, asking the right questions, and adopting the correct mental frame are important steps.

Treat machine learning as if it's human

Executives need to think of machine learning as a living entity, not an inanimate technology. Just as cognitive testing of employees won't reveal how they'll do when added to a preexisting team in a business, laboratory testing cannot predict the performance of machine-learning systems in the real world. Executives should demand a full analysis of how employees, customers, or other users will apply these systems and react to their decisions. Even when not required to do so by regulators, companies may want to subject their new machine-learning-based products to randomized controlled trials to ensure their safety, efficacy, and fairness prior to rollout. But they may also want to analyze products' decisions in the actual market, where there are various types of users, to see whether the quality of decisions differs across them. In addition, companies should compare the quality of decisions made by the algorithms with those made in the same situations *without* employing them. Before deploying products at scale, especially but not only those that haven't undergone randomized controlled trials, companies should consider testing them in limited markets to get a better idea of their accuracy and behavior when various factors are at play—for instance, when users don't have equal expertise, the data from sources varies, or the environment changes. Failures in real-world settings signal the need to improve or retire algorithms.

Think like a regulator and certify first

Businesses should develop plans for certifying machine-learning offerings before they go to market. The practices of regulators offer a good road map. In 2019, for example, the FDA published a discussion paper that proposed a new regulatory framework for modifications to machine-learning-based software as a medical device. It laid out an approach that would allow such software to continuously improve while maintaining the safety of patients, which included a complete assessment of the company—or team—developing the software to ensure it had a culture of organizational excellence and high quality that would lead it to regularly test its machine-learning devices. If companies don't adopt such certification processes, they may expose themselves to liability—for example, for performing insufficient due diligence.

Many start-ups provide services to certify that products and processes don't suffer from bias, prejudice, stereotypes, unfairness, and other pitfalls. Professional organizations, such as the Institute of Electrical and Electronics Engineers and the International Organization for Standardization, are also developing standards for such certification, while companies like Google offer AI ethics services that examine multiple dimensions, ranging from the data used to train systems, to their behavior, to their impact on well-being. Companies might need to develop similar frameworks of their own.

Monitor continuously

As machine-learning-based products and services and the environments they operate in evolve, companies may find that their technologies don't perform as initially intended. It is therefore important that they set up ways to check that these technologies behave within appropriate limits. Other sectors can serve as models. The FDA's Sentinel Initiative draws from disparate data sources, such as electronic health records, to monitor the safety of medical products and can force them to be withdrawn if they don't pass muster. In many ways companies' monitoring programs may be similar to the preventive maintenance tools and processes currently used by manufacturing or energy companies or in cybersecurity. For example, firms might conduct so-called adversarial attacks on AI like those used to routinely test the strength of IT systems' defenses.

Ask the right questions

Executives and regulators need to delve into the following:

Accuracy and competitiveness. How much is the performance of the machine-learning-based system likely to improve with the volume of new data from its use if we don't lock the algorithm? What will such improvements mean for the business? To what extent will consumers understand the benefits and drawbacks of locked versus unlocked systems?

Biases. What data was used to train the algorithm? How representative is it of the population on which the algorithm will ultimately operate? Can we predict whether an unlocked algorithm will produce less-biased results than a locked one if we allow it to learn over time? Do the algorithm's errors affect minorities or other groups in particular? Can a continuous monitoring approach establish "guardrails" that stop the algorithm from becoming discriminatory?

The environment. How will the environment in which the offering is used change over time? Are there conditions under which machine learning should not be allowed to make decisions, and if so, what are they? How can we ensure that the offering's behavior evolves appropriately given how the environment itself is changing?

When should we withdraw our offering because the gap between the environment and our offering's behavior has become too big? What are the boundaries of the environment within which our offering can adapt and operate? How robust and safe are our machine-learning systems throughout their life cycles?

Agency. On which third-party components, including data sources, does the behavior of our machine-learning algorithms depend? How much does it vary when they're used by different types of people—for example, less-skilled ones? What products or services of other organizations use our data or machine-learning algorithms, possibly exposing us to liability? Should we allow other organizations to use machine-learning algorithms that we develop?

Develop principles that address your business risks

Businesses will need to establish their own guidelines, including ethical ones, to manage these new risks—as some companies, like Google and Microsoft, have already done. Such guidelines often need to be quite specific (for example, about what definitions of fairness are adopted) to be useful and must be tailored to the risks in question. If you're using machine learning to make hiring decisions, it would be good to have a model that is simple, fair, and transparent. If you're using machine learning to forecast the prices of commodity futures contracts, you may care less about those values and more about the maximum potential financial loss allowed for any decision that machine learning makes.

Luckily, the journey to develop and implement principles doesn't need to be a lonely one. Executives have a lot to learn from the multiyear efforts of institutions such as the OECD, which developed the first intergovernmental AI principles (adopted in 2019 by many countries). The OECD principles promote innovative, trustworthy, and responsibly transparent AI that respects human rights, the rule of law, diversity, and democratic values, and that drives inclusive growth, sustainable development, and well-being. They also emphasize the robustness, safety, security, and continuous risk management of AI systems throughout their life cycles.

The OECD's recently launched AI Policy Observatory provides further useful resources, such as a comprehensive compilation of AI policies around the world.

———————

Machine learning has tremendous potential. But as this technology, along with other forms of AI, is woven into our economic and social fabric, the risks it poses will increase. For businesses, mitigating them may prove as important as—and possibly more critical than—managing the adoption of machine learning itself. If companies don't establish appropriate practices to address these new risks, they're likely to have trouble gaining traction in the marketplace.

Originally published in January–February 2021. Reprint R2101F

Getting Serious About Diversity

by Robin J. Ely and David A. Thomas

THESE RALLYING CRIES for more diversity in companies, from recent statements by CEOs, are representative of what we hear from business leaders around the world. They have three things in common: All articulate a business case for hiring more women or people of color; all demonstrate good intentions; and none of the claims is actually supported by robust research findings.

We say this as scholars who were among the first to demonstrate the potential benefits of more race and gender heterogeneity in organizations. In 1996 we published an HBR article, "Making Differences Matter: A New Paradigm for Managing Diversity," in which we argued that companies adopting a radically new way of understanding and leveraging diversity could reap the real and full benefits of a diverse workforce. This new way entailed not only recruiting and retaining more people from underrepresented "identity groups" but also tapping their identity-related knowledge and experiences as resources for learning how the organization could perform its core work better. Our research showed that when companies take this approach, their teams are more effective than either homogeneous teams or diverse teams that don't learn from their members' differences. Such companies send a message that varied points of view are valued and don't need to be suppressed for the sake of group cohesion. This attitude encourages employees to rethink how work gets done and how best to achieve their goals.

We called this approach the *learning-and-effectiveness paradigm*. We argued that cultivating a learning orientation toward diversity—one in which people draw on their experiences as members of particular identity groups to reconceive tasks, products, business processes, and organizational norms—enables companies to increase their effectiveness. We stand by the research on which that article was based, and we continue to advocate its conclusions.

The problem is that nearly 25 years later, organizations have largely failed to adopt a learning orientation toward diversity and are no closer to reaping its benefits. Instead, business leaders and diversity advocates alike are advancing a simplistic and empirically unsubstantiated version of the business case. They misconstrue or ignore what abundant research has now made clear: Increasing the numbers of traditionally underrepresented people in your workforce does not *automatically* produce benefits. Taking an "add diversity and stir" approach, while business continues as usual, will not spur leaps in your firm's effectiveness or financial performance.

And despite all the rhetoric about the value of diversity, white women and people of color remain seriously underrepresented in many industries and in most companies' senior ranks. That lack of progress suggests that top executives don't actually find the business case terribly compelling.

On that point, we have to agree: The *simplistic* business case isn't persuasive. A credible and powerful case *can* be made, however, with three critical modifications. First, platitudes must give way to sound, empirically based conclusions. Second, business leaders must reject the notion that maximizing shareholder returns is paramount; instead they must embrace a broader vision of success that encompasses learning, innovation, creativity, flexibility, equity, and human dignity. Finally, leaders must acknowledge that increasing demographic diversity does not, by itself, increase effectiveness; what matters is how an organization harnesses diversity, and whether it's willing to reshape its power structure.

In this article we expose the flaws in the current diversity rhetoric and then outline what a 21st-century learning-and-effectiveness paradigm could look like—and how leaders can foster it.

Idea in Brief

The Context

Business leaders often make a business case for diversity, claiming that hiring more women or people of color results in better financial performance.

The Problem

There's no empirical evidence that simply diversifying the workforce, absent fundamental changes to the organizational culture, makes a company more profitable.

A Better Approach

Companies *can* benefit from diversity if leaders create a psychologically safe workplace, combat systems of discrimination and subordination, embrace the styles of employees from different identity groups, and make cultural differences a resource for learning and improving organizational effectiveness.

A Critique of the Business Case for Diversity

Let's start with the claim that putting more women on corporate boards leads to economic gains. That's a fallacy, probably fueled by studies that went viral a decade ago reporting that the more women directors a company has, the better its financial performance. But those studies show correlations, not causality. In all likelihood, some other factor—such as industry or firm size—is responsible for both increases in the number of women directors and improvement in a firm's performance.

In any case, the research touting the link was conducted by consulting firms and financial institutions and fails to pass muster when subjected to scholarly scrutiny. Meta-analyses of rigorous, peer-reviewed studies found no significant relationships—causal or otherwise—between board gender diversity and firm performance. That could be because women directors may not differ from their male counterparts in the characteristics presumed to affect board decisions, and even if they do differ, their voices may be marginalized. What is more pertinent, however, is that board decisions are typically too far removed from firms' bottom-line performance to exert a direct or unconditional effect.

As for studies citing the positive impact of racial diversity on corporate financial performance, they do not stand up to scrutiny either. Indeed, we know of no evidence to suggest that replacing, say, two or three white male directors with people from underrepresented groups is likely to enhance the profits of a *Fortune* 500 company.

The economic argument for diversity is no more valid when it's applied to changing the makeup of the overall workforce. A 2015 survey of Harvard Business School alumni revealed that 76% of those in senior executive positions believe that "a more diverse workforce improves the organization's financial performance." But scholarly researchers have rarely found that increased diversity leads to improved financial outcomes. They *have* found that it leads to higher-quality work, better decision-making, greater team satisfaction, and more equality—under certain circumstances. Although those outcomes could conceivably make some aspects of the business more profitable, they would need to be extraordinarily consequential to affect a firm's bottom line.

Moreover, advocates who justify diversity initiatives on the basis of financial benefits may be shooting themselves in the foot. Research suggests that when company diversity statements emphasize the economic payoffs, people from underrepresented groups start questioning whether the organization is a place where they really belong, which reduces their interest in joining it. In addition, when diversity initiatives promise financial gains but fail to deliver, people are likely to withdraw their support for them.

Still another flaw in the familiar business case for diversity is the notion that a diverse team will have richer discussions and a better decision-making process simply because it is diverse. Having people from various identity groups "at the table" is no guarantee that anything will get better; in fact, research shows that things often get worse, because increasing diversity can increase tensions and conflict. Under the right organizational conditions, though, employees can turn cultural differences into assets for achieving team goals.

Studies have shown, for example, that diverse teams realize performance benefits in certain circumstances: when team members are able to reflect on and discuss team functioning; when status differences among ethnic groups are minimized; when people from both high- and low-status identity groups believe the team supports learning; and—as we reported in our earlier article—when teams orient members to learn from their differences rather than marginalize or deny them. But absent conditions that foster inquiry, egalitarianism, and learning, diversity either is unrelated to or undermines team effectiveness.

Many progressive companies today recognize the conditional nature of the diversity-performance link and have moved beyond "diversity," the catchword of the 1990s, to "diversity and inclusion." They understand that just increasing the number of people from underrepresented groups is not meaningful if those employees do not feel valued and respected. We applaud the emphasis on inclusion, but it is insufficient because it doesn't fundamentally reconfigure power relations.

Being genuinely valued and respected involves more than just feeling included. It involves having the power to help set the agenda, influence what—and how—work is done, have one's needs and interests taken into account, and have one's contributions recognized and rewarded with further opportunities to contribute and advance. Undertaking this shift in power is what the learning-and-effectiveness companies we wrote about in 1996 were doing, and it's what enabled them to tap diversity's true benefits.

The Learning-and-Effectiveness Paradigm, Redux

What we've learned since we wrote our original article is that embracing a learning orientation toward diversity turns out to be quite difficult. To make real progress, people—and the organizational cultures they inhabit—must change. But instead of doing the·hard work involved, companies have generally stuck with easier, more limited approaches that don't alter the status quo.

We previously identified four actions that were helping business leaders and managers shift to a learning-and-effectiveness approach. We still consider those actions fundamental, but we present them anew here to underscore the message in light of today's challenges and opportunities.

Build trust

The first task for those in charge is to build trust by creating a workplace where people feel safe expressing themselves freely. That requires setting a tone of honest discourse and getting comfortable with vulnerability—one's own and others'.

At no time has this need been greater in the United States than during the current unrest spurred by outrage over police brutality against Black men and women—a legacy of centuries of racism. Two weeks into the nationwide protests that began in May, white leaders in companies across the country struggled with how to respond. Publicly expressing support for the Black Lives Matter movement was one thing; knowing what to say to Black employees, who might already have been feeling marginalized or undervalued at work, was quite another. Leaders who were used to wielding authority grounded in their subject-matter expertise had no comparable expertise to handle the deep grief, rage, and despair felt by many of their employees—especially their Black employees. And Black leaders, many with firsthand experience of police mistreatment and other forms of racial oppression, faced the challenge of managing their own strong emotions and speaking their truth without appearing biased against whites.

Yet troubling times provide opportunities for leaders to begin conversations that foster learning. In response to public acts of racial injustice, for example, white leaders can reach out from a place of vulnerability, as a way of creating connection and psychological safety, rather than staying silent from a place of privilege and self-protection. This was the choice made by a white senior partner in a global professional services firm when he decided to convene a special virtual meeting with his teams across the country. He knew that if he said nothing about the recent racist incidents, his silence would speak for him, with a message not of neutrality but of complicity. Just weeks before, he'd been eloquent in addressing the distress wrought by the Covid-19 pandemic, but when it came to race, he felt at a complete loss. What he astutely realized, though, was that people needed him simply to begin a dialogue, acknowledge his pain and theirs, and give them the space to talk about their experiences inside and outside the firm, if they wished. He had no solutions, but that moment required none—just a willingness to speak from the heart and listen compassionately to whatever his colleagues might share. Perhaps most important, he was willing to risk not getting his own words or actions exactly right, and he was ready to receive feedback with openness and equanimity.

Actively work against discrimination and subordination

Creating psychological safety and building employees' trust can be an excellent starting point for the second action: taking concrete measures to combat forms of discrimination and subordination that inhibit employees' ability to thrive. This action calls for both individual and collective learning aimed at producing systemic change.

Over the years we've seen the emergence of a multibillion-dollar industry dedicated to advancing such goals. Companies have adopted a slew of initiatives as a result: affinity groups, mentoring programs, work-family accommodation policies, and unconscious-bias training, to name a few. But the sad truth is that these efforts largely fail to produce meaningful, sustained change—and sometimes even backfire.

Leaders are the stewards of an organization's culture; their behaviors and mindsets reverberate throughout the organization. Hence to dismantle systems of discrimination and subordination, leaders must undergo the same shifts of heart, mind, and behavior that they want for the organization as a whole and then translate those personal shifts into real, lasting change in their companies.

To that end, a first step for leaders is to learn about how systems of privilege and oppression—racism, sexism, ethnocentrism, classism, heterosexism—operate in the wider culture. Numerous excellent books and articles can help with this work; they have the added benefit of relieving those on the receiving end of oppressive systems from the burden of educating their majority-group counterparts. And the impact can be surprising. For example, major news organizations picked up the story of a Black flight attendant who noticed a white male passenger reading a book about white people's reluctance to confront racism. She struck up a conversation with the man and had a moving exchange with him, eventually learning that he was the CEO of a major airline. The encounter filled her with hope: Here was a powerful executive—someone in a position to effect change—making a genuine effort to understand systemic racism.

Educating oneself is important, but it will be meaningless unless leaders take the next step: investigating how their organization's culture has reproduced systems of oppression, undercutting some groups' opportunities to thrive and succeed, while giving others a boost. As part of that investigation, leaders must examine what stereotypes and assumptions they hold about employees' competencies and suitability for jobs, acknowledge that they have blind spots, and come to see how their personal defenses can shut down learning—their own and their organization's. Working with hundreds of leaders over the years, we have seen how this individual learning journey can be a transformational experience that often leads to individual behavioral change.

But that's not enough. The critical final step in rooting out systems of discrimination and subordination is for leaders to use their personal experience to spur collective learning and systemic change. It is here that even the most progressive leaders' efforts tend to stall. Such efforts require a well-articulated, widely shared organizational mission to motivate and guide change, together with a collective process of continuous reflection and consciousness-raising, experimentation, and action—followed by sustained attention, monitoring each change for impact, and making adjustments accordingly.

An example of this process comes from a midsize consulting firm whose partners—almost all white men—had begun to fear that high turnover among the white women and people of color they employed meant they were losing talent, potentially undermining the firm's competitiveness. Taking a hard look at their culture, they identified a flawed approach to project assignment that was inadvertently contributing to systematic inequities. Plum projects were going disproportionately to white men; it was the old story of people having an easier time identifying talent when it comes in a package that looks like them. When a particularly challenging project for an important client came up—the kind that can stretch and give exposure to a promising young consultant—the white male partners staffed it with their go-to people: other white men. Meanwhile, white women and people of color, despite having been recruited from the same highly competitive MBA programs as their white male counterparts, regularly were assigned the more mundane projects. They got stuck doing tasks they had long ago mastered, which led many to leave the firm. Come promotion time, the few who remained were either counseled out or told they still weren't ready for partnership; women waited two years longer than men, on average, to make partner.

But were the go-to people actually better? Did they really have more "raw horsepower," as the partners believed? When those leaders examined their developmental practices, they were chagrined to see clear patterns in who received coaching, whose mistakes were forgiven, and who got second and even third chances to prove themselves: the white men. So after an uncomfortable reckoning with their biases, the partners decided to experiment with making comparable investments in people they'd previously overlooked— people they might have automatically, if not quite consciously, written off simply as hires to meet diversity goals. When they started treating white women and people of color more like the white men they'd favored, they were surprised to find a bigger, more diverse pool of talent than they'd expected.

Embrace a wide range of styles and voices

The third necessary action for leaders and managers involves actively trying to understand how organizational norms might implicitly discourage certain behavioral styles or silence certain voices. For example, in companies where the prototypical leader is a white man who earns respect by speaking assertively, women and Black men, who are often penalized for being assertive, may find themselves in a double bind: They can conform to the organization's norms and deviate from cultural prescriptions for their group, or they can do the opposite. But either way, they violate one set of expectations, risking marginalization and diminished chances for advancement.

Managers may believe they're giving helpful feedback when they tell a large Black man to smile more so that his white colleagues won't fear him, when they ask a Latina who advocates passionately for a project to dial it down, when they encourage a no-nonsense white woman to be "nicer," or when they urge a soft-spoken woman of East Asian descent to speak more forcefully. But all such messages communicate that these employees must be ever-mindful of how others see them in relation to stereotyped images of their group, making it harder for them to bring their talents and perspectives to the table. Companies need performance management systems that tie feedback and evaluation criteria to bona fide task requirements rather than group stereotypes.

Make cultural differences a resource for learning

For companies shifting to a learning-and-effectiveness paradigm, the fourth action is to encourage—and draw lessons from—open discussions about how identity groups shape employees' experiences inside and outside the organization. Leaders should frame those experiences as a valid source of ideas for enhancing the organization's work and culture. Even if employees champion ideas that are at odds with the company's profit goals, those ideas may still be worth pursuing if they help the organization achieve its mission or uphold its values.

Over the years, we have seen that learning from cultural differences is more likely to occur once the previous three actions are under way: Leaders have created trust, begun to dismantle systems of discrimination and subordination, and embraced a broad range of styles. Without such efforts, talking about differences happens (if it happens at all) only in reaction to diversity-related crises—when discussions tend to be fraught and people's capacity to learn is diminished.

An example of learning from gender diversity comes from Boris Groysberg's study of top-ranked research analysts on Wall Street. In exploring whether they take their star status with them when they switch firms, he found a fascinating sex difference: Unlike their male counterparts, whose performance worsened upon changing firms, women who made a move experienced no such performance drop. The reason, Groysberg concluded, was that women analysts faced sex discrimination, and so they had to do the job differently from men. Women had a more difficult time building support networks inside their firm, had fewer mentors, and were neglected by high-status groups such as the firm's institutional sales force—an important source of industry information. And so, unlike men, women built their franchises on portable, external relationships with clients, companies, and the media. In addition, they forged unconventional in-house relationships with their firm's retail sales force—also an important source of industry information but a low-status group that male analysts typically ignored. Not only were women stars able to maintain their performance upon switching firms but, generally speaking, they outperformed their male peers over the nine-year period of the study. In short, women were not only different; they were better.

In a follow-up set of case studies, coauthored with Ashish Nanda and Laura Morgan Roberts, respectively, Groysberg showed how a Wall Street firm's research director leveraged women's "difference" to everyone's advantage. He aggressively recruited talented women for the analyst role and then set out to create the conditions that would enable them to thrive, emphasizing team culture, allowing flexible work arrangements, and instituting systems that gave analysts regular, unbiased feedback to help them set personal improvement goals. Additionally, he encouraged people to develop their own style and voice. As one woman star in the firm noted, "We have always been given the freedom to be ourselves." Another said, "I never felt I had to pretend to be male to fit in here." Within three years this firm had the highest percentage of top-ranked women analysts of any firm on Wall Street and the lowest rate of female turnover. Furthermore, the research department moved in the rankings from 15th to first, and the unique approach that women had developed for building their franchises became the basis for training all the firm's analysts. What the research director figured out was that gender had given women analysts a unique set of experiences, and those, together with their resilience and ingenuity, led to new insights into how to do the job better.

We have also seen how the mere act of learning across employees' differences can have a positive impact, even when the content of the learning is unrelated to people's identities. The benefits are particularly strong when the differences have been historically fraught with tension. In a study of more than 400 retail bank branches in the northeastern United States, we, together with Irene Padavic of Florida State University, found that the more racially diverse the branch, the better its performance—but only for branches in which *all* employees, across all racial groups, experienced the environment as conducive to learning. Some of that learning definitely came from sharing cultural knowledge—for example, a white branch manager described how his Chinese coworker's explanations of norms in the Chinese community helped him better serve that segment of customers. But many of the branches' tasks were technical and unrelated to people's cultural backgrounds. In those cases, the benefit from diversity seemed to stem mainly from the process of learning—a process that involves taking risks and being unafraid to say "I don't know," "I made a mistake," or "I need help." Showing such vulnerability across divisive lines of difference, such as race, and being met with acceptance rather than judgment or rejection, strengthens relationships. Stronger relationships in turn increase resilience in the face of conflict and other stressors. In short, for culturally diverse teams, the experience of learning across racial differences can, in and of itself, improve performance.

Inequality is bad for both business and society. Organizations limit their capacity for innovation and continuous improvement unless all employees are full participants in the enterprise: fully seen, heard, developed, engaged—and rewarded accordingly. Moreover, such treatment can unleash enormous reserves of leadership potential too long suppressed by systems that perpetuate inequality.

When the only legitimate conversation about diversity is one that links it to economic gains, we tend to discount the problem of inequality. In fact, studies have shown that making the economic case diminishes people's sense that equality is itself important, limits socially conscious investors' ability to promote it, and may even increase bias. Furthermore, focusing on financial benefits sends a message to traditionally underrepresented employees that they are worth hiring and investing in only because having "their kind" in the mix increases the firm's profitability.

Companies will not reap benefits from diversity unless they build a culture that insists on equality. Treating differences as a source of knowledge and connection lays the groundwork for such a culture. But as part of that process, firms may have to make financial investments that they won't recoup, at least in the short run, and more will be required of top leaders, managers, and rank-and-file employees alike. Everyone will have to learn how to actively listen to others' perspectives, have difficult conversations, refrain from blame and judgment, and solicit feedback about how their behaviors and company practices might be impeding the push for a culture that supports learning, equality, and mutual respect. Developing those capacities is no small feat in any context; it is even more challenging for people working across cultural identity differences. But teams that truly embrace the learning-and-effectiveness paradigm will come to understand that homogeneity isn't better; it's just easier. They'll realize, too, that the benefits of diversity arise as much from the collective work of developing those key capacities as from the collective learning they enable.

Finally, while there *is* a business case for diversity—one that rests on sound evidence, an expansive definition of what makes a business successful, and the presence of facilitating conditions—we are disturbed by the implication that there must be economic grounds to justify investing in people from underrepresented groups. Why should anyone need an economic rationale for affirming the agency and dignity of any group of human beings? We should make the necessary investment because doing so honors our own and others' humanity and gives our lives meaning. If company profits come at the price of our humanity, they are costing us too much. And if diversity initiatives fail to reckon with that trade-off, they will amount to little more than rearranging the deck chairs on a sinking ship.

Originally published in November–December 2020. Reprint R2006J

How to Promote Racial Equity in the Workplace

by Robert Livingston

INTRACTABLE AS IT SEEMS, the problem of racism in the workplace can be effectively addressed with the right information, incentives, and investment. Corporate leaders may not be able to change the world, but they can certainly change *their* world.

Organizations are relatively small, autonomous entities that afford leaders a high level of control over cultural norms and procedural rules, making them ideal places to develop policies and practices that promote racial equity. In this article, I'll offer a practical road map for making profound and sustainable progress toward that goal.

I've devoted much of my academic career to the study of diversity, leadership, and social justice, and over the years I've consulted on these topics with scores of *Fortune* 500 companies, federal agencies, nonprofits, and municipalities. Often, these organizations have called me in because they are in crisis and suffering—they just want a quick fix to stop the pain. But that's akin to asking a physician to write a prescription without first understanding the patient's underlying health condition. Enduring, long-term solutions usually require more than just a pill. Organizations and societies alike must resist the impulse to seek immediate relief for the symptoms, and instead focus on the disease. Otherwise they run the risk of a recurring ailment.

To effectively address racism in your organization, it's important to first build consensus around whether there is a problem (most likely, there is) and, if so, what it is and where it comes from. If many of your employees do not believe that racism against people of color exists in the organization, or if feedback is rising through various communication channels showing that Whites feel that they are the real victims of discrimination, then diversity initiatives will be perceived as the problem, not the solution. This is one of the reasons such initiatives are frequently met with resentment and resistance, often by mid-level managers. Beliefs, not reality, are what determine how employees respond to efforts taken to increase equity. So, the first step is getting everyone on the same page as to what the reality is and why it is a problem for the organization.

But there's much more to the job than just raising awareness. Effective interventions involve many stages, which I've incorpo-

A road map for racial equity

Organizations move through these stages sequentially, first establishing an understanding of the underlying condition, then developing genuine concern, and finally focusing on correcting the problem.

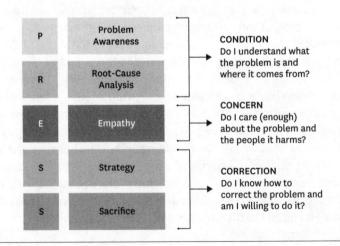

P	Problem Awareness	**CONDITION** Do I understand what the problem is and where it comes from?
R	Root-Cause Analysis	
E	Empathy	**CONCERN** Do I care (enough) about the problem and the people it harms?
S	Strategy	**CORRECTION** Do I know how to correct the problem and am I willing to do it?
S	Sacrifice	

Idea in Brief

The Problem

Racial discrimination—defined as differential evaluation or treatment based solely on race, regardless of intent—remains prevalent in organizations and occurs far more frequently than most White people suspect.

The Opportunity

Intractable as it seems, racism in the workplace can be effectively

addressed. Because organizations are autonomous entities that afford leaders a high level of control over norms and policies, they are ideal places to promote racial equity.

The Way Forward

Effective interventions move through stages, from understanding the underlying condition, to developing genuine concern, to focusing on correction.

rated into a model I call PRESS. The stages, which organizations must move through sequentially, are: (1) Problem awareness, (2) Root-cause analysis, (3) Empathy, or level of concern about the problem and the people it afflicts, (4) Strategies for addressing the problem, and (5) Sacrifice, or willingness to invest the time, energy, and resources necessary for strategy implementation. Organizations going through these stages move from understanding the underlying condition, to developing genuine concern, to focusing on correction.

Let's now have a closer look at these stages and examine how each informs, at a practical level, the process of working toward racial equity.

Problem Awareness

To a lot of people, it may seem obvious that racism continues to oppress people of color. Yet research consistently reveals that many Whites don't see it that way. For example, a 2011 study by Michael Norton and Sam Sommers found that on the whole, whites in the United States believe that systemic anti-Black racism has steadily decreased over the past 50 years—and that systemic anti-White racism (an implausibility in the United States) has steadily increased over the same time frame. The result: As a group, Whites believe that there is more racism against them than against Blacks. Other recent surveys echo Sommers and Norton's findings, one revealing, for example, that 57% of all Whites and 66% of working-class Whites consider discrimination against whites to be as big a problem as discrimination against Blacks and other people of color. These beliefs are important, because they can undermine an organization's efforts to address racism by weakening support for diversity policies. (Interestingly, surveys taken since the George Floyd murder indicate an increase in perceptions of systemic racism among Whites. But it's too soon to tell whether those surveys reflect a permanent shift or a temporary uptick in awareness.)

Even managers who recognize racism in society often fail to see it in their own organizations. For example, one senior executive told me, "We don't have any discriminatory policies in our company." However, it is important to recognize that even seemingly "race neutral" policies can enable discrimination. Other executives point to their organizations' commitment to diversity as evidence for the absence of racial discrimination. "Our firm really values diversity and making this a welcoming and inclusive place for everybody to work," another leader remarked.

Despite these beliefs, many studies in the 21st century have documented that racial discrimination is prevalent in the workplace, and that organizations with strong commitments to diversity are no less likely to discriminate. In fact, research by Cheryl Kaiser and colleagues has demonstrated that the presence of diversity values and structures can actually make matters worse, by lulling an organization into complacency and making Blacks and ethnic minorities more likely to be ignored or harshly treated when they raise valid concerns about racism.

Many White people deny the existence of racism against people of color because they assume that racism is defined by deliberate actions motivated by malice and hatred. However, racism can occur without conscious awareness or intent. When defined simply as differential evaluation or treatment based solely on race, regardless of intent, racism occurs far more frequently than most White people suspect. Let's look at a few examples.

In a well-publicized résumé study by the economists Marianne Bertrand and Sendhil Mullainathan, applicants with White-sounding names (such as Emily Walsh) received, on average, 50% more callbacks for interviews than equally qualified applicants with Black-sounding names (such as Lakisha Washington). The researchers estimated that just being White conferred the same benefit as an additional eight years of work experience—a dramatic head start over equally qualified Black candidates.

Research shows that people of color are well aware of these discriminatory tendencies and sometimes try to counteract them by masking their race. A 2016 study by Sonia Kang and colleagues found that 31% of the Black professionals and 40% of the Asian professionals they interviewed admitted to "Whitening" their résumés, either by adopting a less "ethnic" name or omitting extracurricular experiences (a college club membership, for instance) that might reveal their racial identities.

These findings raise another question: Does Whitening a résumé actually benefit Black and Asian applicants, or does it disadvantage them when applying to organizations seeking to increase diversity? In a follow-up experiment, Kang and her colleagues sent Whitened and non-Whitened résumés of Black or Asian applicants to 1,600 real-world job postings across various industries and geographical areas in the United States. Half of these job postings were from companies that expressed a strong desire to seek diverse candidates. They found that Whitening résumés by altering names and extracurricular experiences increased the callback rate from 10% to nearly 26% for Blacks, and from about 12% to 21% for Asians. What's particularly unsettling is that a company's stated commitment to diversity failed to diminish this preference for Whitened résumés.

This is a very small sample of the many studies that have confirmed the prevalence of racism in the workplace, all of which underscore the fact that people's beliefs and biases must be recognized and addressed as the first step toward progress. Although some leaders acknowledge systemic racism in their organizations and can skip step one, many may need to be convinced that racism persists, despite their "race neutral" policies or pro-diversity statements.

Root-Cause Analysis

Understanding an ailment's roots is critical to choosing the best remedy. Racism can have many psychological sources—cognitive biases, personality characteristics, ideological worldviews, psychological insecurity, perceived threat, or a need for power and ego enhancement. But most racism is the result of structural factors—established laws, institutional practices, and cultural norms. Many of these causes do not involve malicious intent. Nonetheless, managers often misattribute workplace discrimination to the character of individual actors—the so-called bad apples—rather than to broader structural factors. As a result, they roll out trainings to "fix" employees while dedicating relatively little attention to what may be a toxic organizational culture, for example. It is much easier to pinpoint and blame individuals when problems arise. When police departments face crises related to racism, the knee-jerk response is to fire the officers involved or replace the police chief, rather than examining how the culture licenses, or even encourages, discriminatory behavior.

Appealing to circumstances beyond one's control is another way to exonerate deeply embedded cultural or institutional practices that are responsible for racial disparities. For example, an oceanographic organization I worked with attributed its lack of racial diversity to an insurmountable pipeline problem. "There just aren't any Black people out there studying the migration patterns of the humpback whale," one leader commented. Most leaders were unaware of the National Association of Black Scuba Divers, an organization boasting thousands of members, or of Hampton University, a historically Black college on the Chesapeake Bay, which awards bachelor's degrees in marine and environmental science. Both were entities that could source Black candidates for the job, especially given that the organization only needed to fill dozens, not thousands, of openings.

A *Fortune* 500 company I worked with cited similar pipeline problems. Closer examination revealed, however, that the real culprit was the culture-based practice of promoting leaders from within the organization—which already had low diversity—rather than conducting a broader industry-wide search when leadership positions became available. The larger lesson here is that an organization's lack of diversity is often tied to inadequate recruitment efforts rather than an empty pipeline. Progress requires a deeper diagnosis of the routine practices that drive the outcomes leaders wish to change.

To help managers and employees understand how being embedded within a biased system can unwittingly influence outcomes and behaviors, I like to ask them to imagine being fish in a stream. In that stream, a current exerts force on everything in the water, moving it downstream. That current is analogous to systemic racism. If you do nothing—just float—the current will carry you along with it, whether you're aware of it or not. If you actively discriminate by swimming with the current, you will be propelled faster. In both cases, the current takes you in the same direction. From this perspective, racism has less to do with what's in your heart or mind and more to do with how your actions or inactions amplify or enable the systemic dynamics already in place.

Workplace discrimination often comes from well-educated, well-intentioned, open-minded, kindhearted people who are just floating along, severely underestimating the tug of the prevailing current on their actions, positions, and outcomes. Anti-racism requires swimming against that current, like a salmon making its way upstream. It demands much more effort, courage, and determination than simply going with the flow.

In short, organizations must be mindful of the "current," or the structural dynamics that permeate the system, not just the "fish," or individual actors that operate within it.

Empathy

Once people are aware of the problem and its underlying causes, the next question is whether they care enough to do something about it. There is a difference between sympathy and empathy. Many White people experience sympathy, or pity, when they witness racism. But what's more likely to lead to action in confronting the problem is empathy—experiencing the same hurt and anger that people of color are feeling. People of color want solidarity—and social justice—not sympathy, which simply quiets the symptoms while perpetuating the disease.

One way to increase empathy is through exposure and education. The video of George Floyd's murder exposed people to the ugly reality of racism in a visceral, protracted, and undeniable way. Similarly, in the 1960s, northern Whites witnessed innocent Black protesters being beaten with batons and blasted with fire hoses on television. What best prompts people in an organization to register concern about racism in their midst, I've found, are the moments when their non-White coworkers share vivid, detailed accounts of the negative impact that racism has on their lives. Managers can raise awareness and empathy through psychologically safe listening sessions—for employees who want to share their experiences, without feeling obligated to do so—supplemented by education and experiences that provide historical and scientific evidence of the persistence of racism.

For example, I spoke with Mike Kaufmann, CEO of Cardinal Health—the 16th largest corporation in America—who credited a visit to the Equal Justice Initiative's National Memorial for Peace and Justice, in Montgomery, Alabama, as a pivotal moment for the company. While diversity and inclusion initiatives have been a priority for Mike and his leadership team for well over a decade, their focus and conversations related to racial inclusion increased significantly during 2019. As he expressed to me, "Some Americans think when slavery ended in the 1860s that African Americans have had an equal opportunity ever since. That's just not true. Institutional systemic racism is still very much alive today; it's never gone away." Kaufmann is planning a comprehensive education program, which will include a trip for executives and other employees to visit the museum, because he is convinced that the experience will change hearts, open eyes, and drive action and behavioral change.

Empathy is critical for making progress toward racial equity because it affects whether individuals or organizations take any action and if so, what kind of action they take. There are at least four ways to respond to racism: join in and add to the injury, ignore it and mind your own business, experience sympathy and bake cookies for the victim, or experience empathic outrage and take measures to promote equal justice. The personal values of individual employees and the core values of the organization are two factors that affect which actions are undertaken.

Strategy

After the foundation has been laid, it's finally time for the "what do we do about it" stage. Most actionable strategies for change address three distinct but interconnected categories: personal attitudes, informal cultural norms, and formal institutional policies.

To most effectively combat discrimination in the workplace, leaders should consider how they can run interventions on all three of these fronts simultaneously. Focusing only on one is likely to be ineffective and could even backfire. For example, implementing institutional diversity policies without any attempt to create buy-in from employees is likely to produce a backlash. Likewise, focusing just on changing attitudes without also establishing institutional policies that hold people accountable for their decisions and actions may generate little behavioral change among those who don't agree with the policies. Establishing an anti-racist organizational culture, tied to core values and modeled by behavior from the CEO and other top leaders at the company, can influence both individual attitudes and institutional policies.

Just as there is no shortage of effective strategies for losing weight or promoting environmental sustainability, there are ample strategies for reducing racial bias at the individual, cultural, and institutional levels. The hard part is getting people to actually adopt them. Even the best strategies are worthless without implementation.

I'll discuss how to increase commitment to execution in the final section. But before I do, I want to give a specific example of an institutional strategy that works. It comes from Massport, a public organization that owns Boston Logan International Airport and commercial lots worth billions of dollars. When its leaders decided they wanted to increase diversity and inclusion in real estate development in Boston's booming Seaport District, they decided to leverage their land to do it. Massport's leaders made formal changes to the selection criteria determining who is awarded lucrative contracts to build and operate hotels and other large commercial buildings on their parcels. In addition to evaluating three traditional criteria—the developer's experience and financial capital, Massport's revenue potential, and the project's architectural design—they added a fourth criterion called "comprehensive diversity and inclusion," which accounted for 25% of the proposal's overall score, the same as the other three. This forced developers not only to think more deeply about how to create diversity but also to go out and do it. Similarly, organizations can integrate diversity and inclusion into managers' scorecards for raises and promotions—if they think it's important enough. I've found that the real barrier to diversity is not figuring out "What can we do?" but rather "Are we willing to do it?"

Sacrifice

Many organizations that desire greater diversity, equity, and inclusion may not be willing to invest the time, energy, resources, and commitment necessary to make it happen. Actions are often inhibited by the assumption that achieving one desired goal requires sacrificing another desired goal. But that's not always the case. Although nothing worth having is completely free, racial equity often costs less than people may assume. Seemingly conflicting goals or competing commitments are often relatively easy to reconcile—once the underlying assumptions have been identified.

As a society, are we sacrificing public safety and social order when police routinely treat people of color with compassion and respect? No. In fact, it's possible that kinder policing will actually increase public safety. Famously, the city of Camden, New Jersey, witnessed a 40% drop in violent crime after it reformed its police department, in 2012, and put a much greater emphasis on community policing.

The assumptions of sacrifice have enormous implications for the hiring and promotion of diverse talent, for at least two reasons. First, people often assume that increasing diversity means sacrificing principles of fairness and merit, because it requires giving "special" favors to people of color rather than treating everyone the same.

People often assume that fairness means treating everyone *equally*, or exactly the same. In reality, fairness requires treating people equitably—which may entail treating people differently, but in a way that makes sense.

Of course, what is "sensible" depends on the context and the perceiver. Does it make sense for someone with a physical disability to have a parking space closer to a building? Is it fair for new parents to have six weeks of paid leave to be able to care for their baby? Is it right to allow active-duty military personnel to board an airplane early to express gratitude for their service? My answer is yes to all three questions, but not everyone will agree. For this reason, equity presents a greater challenge to gaining consensus than equality.

In thinking about fairness in the context of American society, leaders must consider the unlevel playing fields and other barriers that exist—provided they are aware of systemic racism. They must also have the courage to make difficult or controversial calls. For example, it might make sense to have an employee resource group for Black employees but not white employees. Fair outcomes may require a process of treating people differently. To be clear, different treatment is not the same as "special" treatment—the latter is tied to favoritism, not equity.

One leader who understands the difference is Maria Klawe, the president of Harvey Mudd College. She concluded that the only way to increase the representation of women in computer science was to treat men and women differently. Men and women tended to have different levels of computing experience prior to entering college—different levels of *experience*, not intelligence or potential. Society treats boys and girls differently throughout secondary school—encouraging STEM subjects for boys but liberal arts subjects for girls, creating gaps in experience. To compensate for this gap created by bias in society, the college designed two introductory computer-science tracks—one for students with no computing experience and one for students with some computing experience in high school. The no-experience course tended to be 50% women whereas the some-experience course was predominantly men. By the end of the semester, the students in both courses were on par with one another. Through this and other equity-based interventions, Klawe and her team were able to dramatically increase the representation of women and minority computer-science majors and graduates.

The second assumption many people have is that increasing diversity requires sacrificing high quality and standards. Consider again the fence scenario. All three people have the same height or "potential." What varies is the level of the field and the fence—apt metaphors for privilege and discrimination, respectively. Because the person on the far left has lower barriers to access, does it make sense to treat the other two people differently to compensate? Do we have an obligation to do so when differences in outcomes are caused by the field and the fence, not someone's height? Maria Klawe sure thought so. How much human potential is left unrealized within organizations because we do not recognize the barriers that exist?

Finally, it's important to understand that quality is difficult to measure with precision. There is no test, instrument, survey, or interviewing technique that will enable you to invariably predict who the "best candidate" will be. The NFL draft illustrates the difficulty in predicting future job performance: Despite large scouting departments, plentiful video of prior performance, and extensive tryouts, almost half of first round picks turn out to be busts. This may be true for organizations as well. Research by Sheldon Zedeck and colleagues on corporate hiring processes has found that even the best screening or aptitude tests predict only 25% of intended outcomes, and that candidate quality is better reflected by "statistical bands" rather than a strict rank ordering. This means that there may be absolutely no difference in quality between the candidate who scored first out of 50 people and the candidate who scored eighth.

The big takeaway here is that "sacrifice" may actually involve giving up very little. If we look at people within a band of potential and choose the diverse candidate (for example, number eight) over the top scorer, we haven't sacrificed quality at all—statistically speaking—even if people's intuitions lead them to conclude otherwise.

Managers should abandon the notion that a "best candidate" must be found. That kind of search amounts to chasing unicorns. Instead, they should focus on hiring well-qualified people who show good promise, and then should invest time, effort, and resources into helping them reach their potential.

The tragedies and protests we have witnessed this year across the United States have increased public awareness and concern about racism as a persistent problem in our society. The question we now must confront is whether, as a nation, we are willing to do the hard work necessary to change widespread attitudes, assumptions, policies, and practices. Unlike society at large, the workplace very often requires contact and cooperation among people from different racial, ethnic, and cultural backgrounds. Therefore, leaders should host open and candid conversations about how their organizations are doing at each of the five stages of the model—and use their power to *press* for profound and perennial progress.

Originally published in September–October 2020. Reprint R2005D

Our Work-from-Anywhere Future

by Prithwiraj (Raj) Choudhury

BEFORE 2020 A MOVEMENT was brewing within knowledge-work organizations. Personal technology and digital connectivity had advanced so far and so fast that people had begun to ask, "Do we really need to be together, in an office, to do our work?" We got our answer during the pandemic lockdowns. We learned that a great many of us don't in fact need to be colocated with colleagues on-site to do our jobs. Individuals, teams, entire workforces, can perform well while being entirely distributed—and they have. So now we face new questions: Are all-remote or majority-remote organizations the future of knowledge work? Is work from anywhere (WFA) here to stay?

Without question, the model offers notable benefits to companies and their employees. Organizations can reduce or eliminate real estate costs, hire and use talent globally while mitigating immigration issues, and, research indicates, perhaps enjoy productivity gains. Workers get geographic flexibility (that is, live where they prefer to), eliminate commutes, and report better work/life balance. However, concerns persist regarding how WFA affects communication, including brainstorming and problem-solving; knowledge sharing; socialization, camaraderie, and mentoring; performance evaluation and compensation; and data security and regulation.

To better understand how leaders can capture the upside of WFA while overcoming the challenges and avoiding negative outcomes,

I've studied several companies that have embraced all- or majority-remote models. They include the United States Patent and Trademark Office, or USPTO (which has several thousand WFA workers); Tulsa Remote; Tata Consultancy Services, or TCS (a global IT services company that has announced a plan to be 75% remote by 2025); GitLab (the world's largest all-remote company, with 1,300 employees); Zapier (a workflow automation company with more than 300 employees, none of them colocated, around the United States and in 23 other countries); and MobSquad (a Canadian start-up that employs WFA workers).

The Covid-19 crisis has opened senior leaders' minds to the idea of adopting WFA for all or part of their workforces. In addition to TCS, companies including Twitter, Facebook, Shopify, Siemens, and State Bank of India have announced that they will make remote work permanent even after a vaccine is available. Another organization I've studied is BRAC, one of the world's largest NGOs, which is headquartered in Bangladesh. Forced into remote work this year, it is deciding what work model to adopt for the long term.

If your organization is considering a WFA program, transition, or launch, this article can provide a guide.

A Short History of Remote Work

A large-scale transition from traditional, colocated work to remote work arguably began with the adoption of work-from-home (WFH) policies in the 1970s, as soaring gasoline prices caused by the 1973 OPEC oil embargo made commuting more expensive. Those policies allowed people to eschew physical offices in favor of their homes, coworking spaces, or other community locations, such as coffee shops and public libraries, for occasional days, on a regular part-time basis, or full-time, with the expectation that they would come into the office periodically. Workers were often also given control over their schedules, allowing them to make time for school pickups, errands, or midday exercise without being seen as shirking. They saved time by commuting less and tended to take fewer sick days.

Thanks to the advent of personal computers, the internet, email, broadband connectivity, laptops, cell phones, cloud computing, and

Idea in Brief

The Shift

The Covid-19 lockdowns proved that it is not only possible but perhaps preferable for knowledge workers to do their jobs from anywhere. Will this mark a long-term shift into all-remote work?

Benefits and Challenges

Studies show that working from home yields numerous benefits for both individuals and their organizations, most notably in the form of enhanced productivity and engagement. But when all or most employees are remote, challenges arise for communication, knowledge sharing, socialization, performance evaluation, security, and more.

The Research

As more companies adopt work-from-anywhere policies, best practices are emerging. The experiences of GitLab, Tata Consultancy Services, Zapier, and others show how the risks associated with this type of work can be overcome.

videotelephony, the adoption of WFH increased in the 2000s. As the researchers Ravi S. Gajendran and David A. Harrison note in a 2007 article, this trend was accelerated by the need to comply with, for example, the Americans with Disabilities Act of 1990 and mandates of the U.S. Equal Employment Opportunity Commission.

Research has shown performance benefits. A 2015 study by Nicholas Bloom and coauthors found that when employees opted in to WFH policies, their productivity increased by 13%. When, nine months later, the same workers were given a choice between remaining at home and returning to the office, those who chose the former saw even further improvements: They were 22% more productive than they had been before the experiment. This suggests that people should probably determine for themselves the situation (home or office) that fits them best.

In recent years many companies have allowed more employees to work from home. It's true that several prominent corporations, including Yahoo and IBM, had reversed course before the pandemic, asking their employees to resume colocated work in a bid to spur more-effective collaboration. But other organizations—the ones I study—moved toward greater geographic flexibility, allowing some if not all employees, new and old, to work from anywhere, completely untethered to an office. The USPTO is a prime example. Its leaders launched a WFA program in 2012, building on an existing WFH program that mandated workers' physical presence at headquarters, in northern Virginia, at least one day a week. The WFA program, in contrast, requires employees to spend two years at HQ followed by a WFH phase, after which they may live anywhere in the continental United States, provided they're willing to pay out of pocket for periodic travel back to headquarters (totaling no more than 12 days a year). The patent examiners in the program dispersed all across the country, choosing to move closer to family, to better climates, or to places with a lower cost of living.

Most companies that offer WFH or WFA options keep some workers—at the USPTO it's trainees and administrators—at one or more offices. In other words, they are hybrid-remote operations. But the experiment with all-remote work forced by Covid-19 has caused some of these organizations to strategically move toward majority-remote, with fewer than 50% of employees colocated in physical offices. TCS, for example, which employs close to 418,000 people who were traditionally located either on campuses or at client sites around the world, has decided to adopt a 25/25 model: Employees will spend only 25% of their working hours in the office, and at no point will the company have more than 25% of workers colocated. TCS plans to complete this transition in five years.

Even before the crisis, a smaller group of companies had taken this trend a step further, eliminating offices altogether and dispersing everyone, from entry-level associates to the CEO. GitLab embraces this model at scale: Its remote workers span sales, engineering, marketing, personnel management, and executive roles in more than 60 countries.

Exploring the Benefits

I've spent the past five years studying the practices and productivity trends of WFA companies. The upsides—for individuals, companies, and society—are clear. Let me outline them.

For individuals

One striking finding is how greatly workers benefit from these arrangements. Many told me that they regard the freedom to live anywhere in the world as an important plus. For those in dual-career situations, it eases the pain of looking for two jobs in a single location. One patent examiner told me, "I'm a military spouse, which means I live in a world with frequent moves and personal upheavals that prevent many spouses from pursuing lasting careers of their choice. WFA has been the most meaningful telework program I have encountered. It allows me to follow my husband to any U.S. state at a moment's notice and pursue my own aspirations to contribute to my home and society."

Some cited a better quality of life. "WFA has allowed my children to see their grandparents on a regular basis and play with their cousins," I heard from another USPTO employee. "Being closer to family has improved my overall happiness." Others talked about proximity to medical care for children, accommodating their partners, and the ability to enjoy warmer weather, prettier views, and greater recreational opportunities. Millennials in particular seemed captivated by the idea that WFA would allow them to become "digital nomads," traveling the world while still employed. Before the pandemic-related restrictions, some companies, such as Remote Year, were aiming to facilitate that lifestyle, and some countries, such as Estonia and Barbados, have created a new class of employment visa for such workers. As one patent examiner said, "Participation in [WFA] is outstanding for work/life balance. I live in my favorite part of the country . . . I have more time to relax."

Cost of living was another frequent theme. Because the USPTO did not adjust salaries according to where employees chose to live, one patent examiner told me, "I was able to buy a large home in my new location for about a quarter of the cost in northern Virginia." Some localities, such as the state of Vermont and the city of Tulsa, Oklahoma (where Tulsa Remote is located), have made a concerted effort to lure remote workers, touting the local community and lower costs. In San Francisco the average rent on a two-bedroom apartment is $4,128; in Tulsa it's a mere $675.

WFA also helps knowledge workers deal with immigration issues and other restrictions on their ability to secure good jobs. William Kerr, Susie Ma, and I recently studied MobSquad, whose coworking spaces in Halifax, Calgary, and other cities enable talented knowledge workers to bypass the onerous U.S. visa and green card system and instead obtain fast-track work permits from Canada's Global Talent Stream. Thus they can continue serving companies and clients in the United States and other countries while living and paying taxes in Canada.

One engineer we interviewed had come to the United States after graduating from high school in his home country at the age of 12. At age 16 he enrolled at a U.S. university, where he acquired degrees in math, physics, and computer science in three years. By age 19 he was employed at a medical tech company through the optional practical training (OPT) program, but he failed to get an H-1B visa and faced deportation. MobSquad moved him to Calgary, and he kept working with the same employer.

In interviews with female employees at BRAC, I learned that women whose careers were previously limited by cultural taboos against traveling to remote places or delegating housework had been helped by WFA. As one explained, "Earlier I had to wake up early in the morning and cook three meals for my intergenerational family. Working remotely has allowed me to spread out the household work, get extra sleep, and be more productive."

For organizations

My research also uncovered ample organizational benefits from WFA programs. For example, they increase employee engagement— an important metric of success for any company. In 2013, a year after it instituted work from anywhere, the USPTO was ranked highest on the Best Places to Work in the Federal Government survey.

Workers are not only happier but also more productive. When Cirrus Foroughi, Barbara Larson, and I evaluated the USPTO's transition from WFH to WFA, the timing of which happened at random for workers who'd chosen that path, we found that WFA boosted individual productivity by 4.4%, as measured by the number of patents examined each month. The switch also led examiners to exert greater effort. Of course, further research is needed to determine whether WFA generates similar benefits for workers performing different tasks in other team structures and organizations.

Some gains generated by WFA are more obvious. For example, fewer in-office employees means smaller space requirements and reduced real estate costs. The USPTO estimated that increases in remote work in 2015 saved it $38.2 million. WFA programs also hugely expand an organization's potential talent pool to include workers tied to a location far from that of the company. That's a primary reason for the adoption at TCS of what it calls secure borderless workspaces, or SBWs: It wants to ensure that every project is staffed by employees with the right skills, no matter where they are. Rajesh Gopinathan, the CEO, describes this model as "talent on the cloud," while another senior executive says it will potentially allow the company to tap niche labor markets, such as Eastern Europe, that have a large supply of skilled financial analysts and data scientists.

Finally, WFA can reduce attrition. Some USPTO workers explained that because they loved their preferred locales but also recognized the limited job opportunities there, they were motivated to work harder and stay longer with the Patent Office. Leaders at GitLab, too, pointed to employee retention as a positive outcome of the company's decision to be all-remote. The net benefit, they believe, including the productivity increases and property cost savings they've seen, equals $18,000 a year for each worker.

For society

WFA organizations have the potential to reverse the brain drain that often plagues emerging markets, small towns, and rural locations. In fact, Tulsa Remote was established to attract diverse, energetic, community-minded newcomers to a city still healing from historic race riots a century ago. With an offer of $10,000 to relocate to Tulsa, the company attracted more than 10,000 applications for just 250 slots from 2019 to 2020. Obum Ukabam was one of the workers chosen. When he's not busy with his day job as a marketing manager, he mentors and coaches a local high school debate team. Talented newcomers of varied ethnicities are arguably making the city more multicultural. Meanwhile, the transitions at the USPTO and TCS have brought many people back to their hometowns.

Remote work helps the environment as well. In 2018 Americans' commute time averaged 27.1 minutes each way, or about 4.5 hours a week. Eliminating that commute—particularly in places where most people commute by car—generates a significant reduction in emissions. The USPTO estimates that in 2015 its remote workers drove 84 million fewer miles than if they had been traveling to headquarters, reducing carbon emissions by more than 44,000 tons.

Addressing the Concerns

The office—with its meeting rooms and break areas and opportunities for both formal and informal interaction—has been a way of life for so long that it's hard to imagine getting rid of it. And legitimate hurdles exist to making all-remote work not only manageable but successful. However, the Covid-19 all-remote experiment has taught many knowledge-work organizations and their employees that with time and attention, those concerns can be addressed. And in the companies I've studied, several best practices are emerging.

Communication, brainstorming, and problem-solving

When workers are distributed, synchronous communication becomes more difficult. Tools such as Zoom, Skype, Microsoft Teams, and Google Hangouts can help for those working in the same or similar time zones but not for those spread farther apart. In research with Jasmina Chauvin and Tommy Pan Fang, I found that when changing to or from daylight saving time caused a one- to two-hour reduction in business-hour overlap (BHO) between offices of a very large global corporation, the volume of communication fell by 9.2%, primarily among production workers. When BHO was greater, R&D staffers conducted more unplanned synchronous calls. Group meetings are even harder to schedule. Nadia Vatalidis of GitLab's People Operations group says that having team members in Manila,

Nairobi, Johannesburg, Raleigh, and Boulder made finding a time for their weekly group call nearly impossible.

WFA organizations must therefore get comfortable with asynchronous communication, whether through a Slack channel, a customized intracompany portal, or even a shared Google document in which geographically distributed team members write their questions and comments and trust that other team members in distant time zones will respond at the first opportunity. One benefit to this approach is that employees are more likely to share early-stage ideas, plans, and documents and to welcome early feedback; the pressure to present polished work is less than it would be in more formal, synchronous team meetings. GitLab calls this process blameless problem-solving. The company's leaders note that employees accustomed to a culture of emails, phone calls, and meetings may struggle to change old habits; they solve that problem with training during onboarding and beyond. At Zapier, in a program called Zap Pal, each new hire is matched with an experienced buddy who sets up at least one introductory Zoom call and continues to check in throughout the first month. For synchronous brainstorming the company uses video calls and online whiteboards such as Miro, Stormboard, IPEVO Annotator, Limnu, and MURAL but also urges employees to use asynchronous means of problem-solving through Slack channel threads.

Knowledge sharing
This is another challenge for all-remote or majority-remote organizations. Distributed colleagues can't tap one another on the shoulder to ask questions or get help. Research by Robin Cowan, Paul David, and Dominique Foray has postulated that much workplace knowledge is not codified (even when it can be) and instead resides "in people's heads." This is a problem for all organizations, but much more so for those that have embraced WFA. The companies I've studied solve it with transparent and easily accessible documentation. At GitLab all team members have access to a "working handbook," which some describe as "the central repository for how we run the company." It currently consists of 5,000 searchable pages.

All employees are encouraged to add to it and taught how to create a new topic page, edit an existing one, embed video, and so forth. Ahead of meetings, organizers post agendas that link to the relevant sections to allow invitees to read background information and post questions. Afterward recordings of the sessions are posted on Git-Lab's YouTube channel, agendas are edited, and the handbook is updated to reflect any decisions made.

Employees may see the extra work of documentation as a "tax" and balk at the extremely high level of transparency necessary for a WFA organization to thrive. Thorsten Grohsjean and I have argued that senior managers must set an example on these fronts by codifying knowledge and freely sharing information while explaining that these are necessary trade-offs to allow for geographic flexibility.

A related idea is to create transcripts, publicly post slides, and record video seminars, presentations, and meetings to create a repository of such material that individuals can view asynchronously at their convenience. For its 2020 annual meeting, which was forced by the pandemic to go virtual, the Academy of Management curated 1,120 prerecorded sessions, arguably expanding the flow of knowledge to scholars—especially those in emerging markets—far more than would have been possible at the in-person event, which typically happens in North America.

Socialization, camaraderie, and mentoring

Another major worry, cited by managers and workers alike, is the potential for people to feel isolated socially and professionally, disconnected from colleagues and the company itself, particularly in organizations where some people are colocated and some are not. Research by Cecily D. Cooper and Nancy B. Kurland has shown that remote workers often feel cut off from the information flow they would typically get in a physical office. Without in-person check-ins, managers may miss signs of growing burnout or team dysfunction. Even with videoconferencing that allows for reading body language and facial expressions, the concern is that virtual colleagues are less likely to become close friends because their face-to-face interactions are less frequent. As GitLab's technical evangelist Priyanka

Sharma put it, "I was very nervous when I was first thinking of joining, because I was very social in the office. I worried that I would be so lonely at home and wouldn't have that community feel." Houda Elyazgi, a marketing executive on the Tulsa Remote team, expressed similar sentiments: "Remote work can be very isolating, especially for introverts. You almost have to create an intentional experience when you're socializing with others. And then you have to be 'on' all the time, even when you're trying to relax. That's taxing."

In my research I've seen a range of policies that seek to address these concerns and create opportunities for socialization and the spreading of company norms. Many WFA organizations rely on technology to help facilitate virtual watercoolers and "planned randomized interactions," whereby someone in the company schedules groups of employees to chat online. Some use AI and virtual reality tools to pair up remote colleagues for weekly chats. For example, Sike Insights is using data on individual communication styles and AI to create Slackbot buddies, while eXp Realty, an all-remote company I'm currently researching, uses a VR platform called VirBELA to create a place for distant team members to gather in avatar form.

Sid Sijbrandij, a cofounder and the CEO of GitLab, told me, "I know at Pixar they placed the restroom centrally so people would bump into each other—but why depend on randomness for that? Why not step it up a notch and actually organize the informal communication?" These "mixers" often include senior and C-suite executives. When I described them to my HBS colleague Christina Wallace, she gave them a nice name: *community collisions*. And companies have always needed to manufacture them: Research dating back to Thomas J. Allen's work at MIT in the 1970s shows that workers colocated on the same "campus" may not experience serendipitous interactions if they are separated by a wall, a ceiling, or a building.

When it comes to interaction between people at different hierarchical levels, my research has revealed two problems with straightforward solutions. Iavor Bojinov, Ashesh Rambachan, and I found that the senior leaders of a global firm were often too stretched to offer one-on-one mentoring to virtual workers. So we implemented a Q&A process whereby workers posed questions through a survey and leaders responded asynchronously. Senior managers at another global firm told me that they had difficulty being themselves on camera. Whereas young remote workers were "living their lives on Instagram," their older colleagues found virtual engagement harder. The company implemented coaching sessions to make those executives more comfortable on Microsoft Teams.

Another solution to the socialization problem is to host "temporary colocation events," inviting all workers to spend a few days with colleagues in person. Prior to Covid-19, Zapier hosted two of those a year, paying for employee flights, accommodation, and food; giving teams an activities budget; and sending people home with $50 to use on a thank-you gift for their loved ones. Carly Moulton, the company's senior communications specialist, told me, "Personally, I have made a lot of friendships with the people I travel to and from the airport with. The event managers will put us into random groups based on what time you arrive and depart. I've always been with people I don't normally work with, so it's nice to have a dedicated time when you have to make conversation."

Finally, at the USPTO, I learned another way to create camaraderie. Several WFA examiners have voluntarily created "remote communities of practice" so that a handful of them can get together periodically. A group living in North Carolina, for example, decided to schedule meetings on a golf course to socialize, discuss work, and problem-solve together. Another manager created a "virtual meal" by ordering the same pizza for delivery to the homes of all remote direct reports during a weekly team call.

Performance evaluation and compensation
How can you rate and review employees you're never physically with, particularly on "soft" but important metrics such as interpersonal skills? All-remote companies evaluate remote workers according to the quality of their work output, the quality of virtual interactions, and feedback from clients and colleagues. Zapier, for example, uses Help Scout for customer support replies; a feature of this software is that customers can submit a "happiness score" by rating the response as "great," "OK," or "not good."

In the spring and summer of 2020, as groups suddenly transitioned to remote work, I was asked whether managers should use software to track worker productivity and prevent shirking. I am very much opposed to this Orwellian approach. The USPTO addressed claims of "examiner fraud" and "attendance abuse" in its WFA program following a review by the U.S. Commerce Department's Office of the Inspector General. Those claims involved either overreporting of hours worked or shifts in the time logs of completed work, such as backloading at the end of a calendar quarter—neither of which related to the metric on which performance was measured: the number of patents examined. Nevertheless, from then on, all USPTO teleworkers had to use organizational IT tools, such as logging in to a virtual private network (VPN), having a presence indicator turned on, and using the same messaging services. But when we compared data from before and after that intervention, we found that it had no effect on average output.

How to set compensation for workers who work from anywhere is an active and interesting debate. As mentioned, it's a benefit to be able to reside in a lower-cost-of-living locale while earning the income one would in a more expensive one. But that's conditional on the company's not adjusting wages according to where a worker lives, as was the case at the USPTO. Matt Mullenweg, the founder of Automattic (parent of WordPress), another all-remote company, told me that its policy is to pay the same wages for the same roles, regardless of location. But GitLab and other companies do have different pay for different geographies, taking into account the experience of the worker, the contract type, and the task being performed. Although research is needed on which approach is optimal, it's possible that companies that tie wages to location will lose high-quality WFA workers to rivals that don't. Another pertinent issue is whether to pay WFA workers in the currency of the country where the organization is incorporated or the local one, in part to ensure consistent wages across locations over time given exchange-rate fluctuations.

Data security and regulation

Several managers told me that cybersecurity was a big area of focus for WFA programs and organizations. "What if the WFA worker takes photographs of client data screens and sends them to a competitor?" one asked. The CIOs of some companies with remote-work policies said another key concern was employees' use of personal, less-protected devices for work at home.

It's true that all-remote companies have to work harder to protect employee, corporate, and customer data. As TCS transitions to a majority-remote model, it has moved from "perimeter-based security" (whereby the IT team attempts to secure every device) to "transaction-based security" (whereby machine learning algorithms analyze any abnormal activities on any employee laptop). MobSquad has replicated its client security infrastructure for WFA workers, and employees work on clients' cloud, email, and hardware in its offices for security reasons. All-remote and majority-remote organizations I have studied are experimenting with a wide range of solutions to protect client data using predictive analytics, data visualization, and computer vision.

Transitioning to an all-remote or a majority-remote organization sometimes requires jumping regulatory hurdles as well. At the onset of the pandemic, when TCS was forced to become all-remote, it had to work with NASSCOM (India's National Association of Software and Service Companies) and the Indian authorities to change laws overnight so that call center staffers could work from home. Other laws had to be tweaked so that TCS workers could take laptops and other equipment out of physical offices located in India's "special economic zones." Irfhan Rawji, the founder and CEO of MobSquad, had to work closely with the Canadian government to ensure that the economic migrants chosen by the company to move to Canada could receive their expedited work permits and be integrated into its model. Any all-remote organization thinking about hiring talent globally has to consider local labor laws as they relate to hiring, compensation, pensions, vacation, and sick leave.

Is This Right for Your Organization?

Of course, WFA may not be possible at this time for some organizations, such as manufacturing companies—though that could change with advances in 3D printing, automation, digital twins, and other technologies. However, with the right strategy, organizational processes, technologies, and—most important—leadership, many more companies, teams, and functions than one might have thought could go all or mostly remote. My ongoing research with Jan Bena and David Rowat suggests, for example, that start-up knowledge-work companies, particularly in the tech sector, are well positioned to adopt a WFA model from their inception. Take the all-remote eXp Realty: We found that lower real estate, utility, and other overhead costs may mean a higher valuation for the company if and when its founders exit the start-up.

My studies of the USPTO and TCS indicate that large and mature organizations, too, can successfully transition to a hybrid or a majority-remote regime. The question is not whether work from anywhere is possible but what is needed to make it possible. The short answer: management. "If all senior leaders are working from an office, then workers would be drawn to that location to get face time," one all-remote middle manager told me. But if leaders support synchronous and asynchronous communication, brainstorming, and problem-solving; lead initiatives to codify knowledge online; encourage virtual socialization, team building, and mentoring; invest in and enforce data security; work with government stakeholders to ensure regulatory compliance; and set an example by becoming WFA employees themselves, all-remote organizations may indeed emerge as the future of work.

Originally published in November–December 2020. Reprint R2006C

A More Sustainable Supply Chain

by Verónica H. Villena and Dennis A. Gioia

IN RECENT YEARS a rising number of multinational corporations have pledged to work only with suppliers that adhere to social and environmental standards. Typically, these MNCs expect their first-tier suppliers to comply with those standards, and they ask that those suppliers in turn ask for compliance from *their* suppliers—who ideally ask the same from *their* suppliers. And so on. The aim is to create a cascade of sustainable practices that flows smoothly throughout the supply chain, or, as we prefer to call it, the supply network.

It's an admirable idea, but it's been hard to realize in practice. Many of the MNCs that have committed to it have faced scandals brought about by suppliers that, despite being aware of sustainability standards, have nevertheless gone on to violate them. Consider the embarrassing scrutiny that Apple, Dell, and HP endured not long ago for sourcing electronics from overseas companies that required employees to work in hazardous conditions, and the fallout that Nike and Adidas suffered for using suppliers that were dumping toxins into rivers in China.

What's more, all those scandals involved first-tier suppliers. The practices of lower-tier suppliers are almost always worse, increasing companies' exposure to serious financial, social, and environmental risks. In this article we describe various ways that MNCs can defuse the ticking time bomb those risks represent.

About the Research

WE FOCUSED OUR STUDY on three "exemplary" multinational corporations that met five selection criteria: (1) They were included in the Dow Jones Sustainability Index. (2) They were members of the Carbon Disclosure Project (CDP) and the United Nations Global Compact. (3) They had been involved in industrywide supply-chain sustainability efforts. (4) They were certified as having a large percentage of plants with effective quality-management systems (ISO 9001), environmental management systems (ISO 14001), and safety-management systems (OHSAS 18001). (5) They were members of the Billion Dollar Roundtable (firms spending at least $1 billion with minority- and women-owned suppliers).

We also interviewed representatives of industry associations (including the Responsible Business Alliance and the Automotive Industry Action Group) and NGOs (including the CDP and the Centre for Reflection and Action on Labour Rights) to gain a more comprehensive view of how each of these stakeholders helps MNCs disseminate their sustainability agendas throughout their supply networks.

For more information about the research, see "The Missing Link? The Strategic Role of Procurement in Building Sustainable Supply Networks," by Verónica H. Villena, *Production and Operations Management* (May 2019), and "On the Riskiness of Lower-Tier Suppliers: Managing Sustainability in Supply Networks," by Verónica H. Villena and Dennis A. Gioia, *Journal of Operations Management* (November 2018).

Where the Problems Are

To understand the situation and develop ideas for tackling it, we conducted a study of three supply networks. Each was headed by an MNC considered to be a "sustainability leader"—one in the automotive industry, one in electronics, and one in pharmaceuticals and consumer products. (For the specific selection criteria, see the "About the Research" sidebar.) We also studied a representative set of each MNC's suppliers—a total of nine top-tier and 22 lower-tier suppliers, based variously in Mexico, China, Taiwan, and the United States. What we discovered was that many were violating the standards that the MNCs expected them to adhere to. The hoped-for cascade effect was seldom occurring.

We found problems in every country we studied. In Mexico we visited five lower-tier suppliers; all lacked environmental management

Idea in Brief

The Problem

Many multinational corporations have committed themselves to using suppliers with sustainable social and environmental practices, but suppliers—especially those low in the supply chain—often don't comply with standards. This poses serious financial, social, and environmental risks.

The Research

The authors studied the supply networks of three MNCs considered to be sustainability leaders. They discovered a set of best practices—but also saw how difficult it can be to enforce standards.

The Solution

Awareness is key. Companies should consider adopting the best practices featured in this article, such as establishing long-term sustainability goals and including lower-tier suppliers in an overall sustainability strategy.

systems, and four lacked procedures for handling red-flag social problems such as sexual harassment, retaliation by supervisors, and hazardous labor conditions. At three of the companies, temporary workers made up nearly 50% of the workforce, and turnover rates sometimes reached 100%, making it difficult to implement viable environmental, health, and safety programs. In China and Taiwan we visited 10 lower-tier suppliers, all of which had marginal environmental practices, dangerous working conditions, and chronic overtime issues. In the United States we studied seven lower-tier suppliers and found that three had high concentrations of airborne chemicals and a lack of systematic accident reporting.

The pattern is worrisome. Remember, all those suppliers were connected to model firms that were working proactively to encourage sustainability. If exemplary MNCs are having trouble ensuring good practices among their lower-tier suppliers, then "regular" firms, in all likelihood, are faring even worse at this.

The problem, ironically, often starts with the MNCs themselves. They frequently place orders that exceed suppliers' capacity or impose unrealistic deadlines, leading supplier factories to demand heavy overtime from their workers. When we asked a representative at one supplier why his company had violated a 60-hour workweek limit, he gave us a frank explanation: "We didn't want to tell our customer that we can't produce its products on time, because otherwise it's going to try to find someone else that can. But our customer didn't give us enough notice to hire enough skilled people to do the job."

First-tier suppliers, for their part, rarely concern themselves with their own suppliers' sustainability practices. That's often because they're struggling with sustainability issues themselves. The noncompliant company we cited above, for example, doesn't try to enforce a strict 60-hour workweek limit with any of its suppliers. "We don't comply with this requirement ourselves," the representative told us, "so how could we ask our own suppliers to do so?"

For MNCs, there are special challenges in governing lower-tier suppliers. There's often no direct contractual relationship, and a particular MNC's business often doesn't mean that much to the lower-tier supplier. If American and Japanese automakers rely heavily on a certain seat maker, for example, they can demand that it adhere to their sustainability standards. But that seat maker may have a hard time getting *its* suppliers to follow suit. Suppose it does business with a foam manufacturer that has many other big customers in the electronics, appliance, and health care industries—each of which has different sustainability standards. The foam manufacturer has little incentive to conform to the automakers' sustainability requirements, because the automakers account for only a small fraction of its total business.

Furthermore, most lower-tier suppliers are not well known, so they receive relatively little attention and pressure from the media, NGOs, and other stakeholders. Even when they do attract attention (for sexual harassment problems, for example, or chronic overtime demands), we found that they do not feel the need to address the issues involved. They tend to act only when MNCs intervene.

Lower-tier suppliers are also the least equipped to handle sustainability requirements. They often do not have sustainability expertise or resources, and they may be unaware of accepted social and environmental practices and regulations. They are also frequently located in countries where such regulations are nonexistent, lax, or not enforced at all. And typically they don't know much about the sustainability requirements imposed by MNCs—but even if they do, they have no incentive to comply. This may explain why most of the lower-tier suppliers in our study lacked programs to dispose of toxic waste and in fact had no environmental management program whatsoever.

MNCs, too, are handicapped by ignorance. They frequently don't even know who their lower-tier suppliers are, let alone where they're located or what capabilities they have (or don't have). Many of the 22 lower-tier suppliers in our study are small or medium-size private firms that provide little information to the public—characteristics that, in effect, make them almost invisible. Several directors of the three MNCs we studied viewed this as a big problem. "The demon in this place," one of them said, "is the [lower-tier] suppliers that I know the least about." Another said, "I don't have control over the ones that pose the highest risks, so I'm losing sleep over them."

All these concerns mean that lower-tier suppliers are unquestionably the riskiest members of a supply network. If they have poor or dubious sustainability performance, then an MNC that does business with them can endanger its reputation and suffer profound repercussions—losing customers, being forced to find new suppliers, or having its supply chain disrupted. To reduce such risks, MNCs need to include both first-tier and lower-tier suppliers in their sustainability programs.

Best Practices

The three MNCs in our study have taken a number of steps to promote suppliers' social and environmental responsibility:

- They have established long-term sustainability goals.

- They require first-tier suppliers to set their own long-term sustainability goals.

- They include lower-tier suppliers in the overall sustainability strategy.

- They task a point person on staff with extending the firm's sustainability program to first- and lower-tier suppliers.

These are all beneficial measures that other companies should consider adopting. Firms can also borrow some of the specific strategies that our MNCs use to spread good practices throughout their supply networks. (See the exhibit "Managing lower-tier supplier sustainability.") These fall into four broad categories:

Direct approach

The MNCs we studied set and monitor social and environmental targets for their first-tier suppliers regarding second-tier suppliers. The automotive corporation, for instance, has a strong commitment to supplier diversity. It requires its first-tier suppliers to allocate 7% of their procurement spending to minority suppliers. Some first-tier suppliers were already meeting that target; others have made substantial changes to do so (for example, by changing performance criteria for their purchasing managers). The first-tier suppliers we interviewed noted that the MNC periodically checks to see if the target is being met and creates opportunities to help them network with minority lower-tier suppliers.

Another MNC annually surveys its first-tier suppliers to gather information not only about their health, safety, labor, and environmental practices but also about the sustainability performance of their lower-tier suppliers. The surveys seem to be having the desired effect: They've prompted first-tier suppliers to engage in internal discussions about whether they should and could alter their procurement practices (to adopt industrywide sustainability standards, for example). And on two occasions, firms have made changes to comply with MNC requirements (such as using key performance indicators to monitor supplier sustainability).

Additionally, the three MNCs work with their major suppliers to map the connections and interdependencies in their supply networks, including those at the lower-tier level. This allows them to identify potentially risky lower-tier suppliers and to work with the major suppliers to deploy customized risk-mitigation programs where needed.

Indirect approach

The MNCs we studied delegate elements of lower-tier-supplier sustainability management to their first-tier suppliers. This approach

Managing lower-tier supplier sustainability

Ideally, multinational corporations will use a combination of approaches—direct, indirect, collective, and global—to encourage sustainable practices throughout their supply networks. Some specific strategies within each type of approach are listed below.

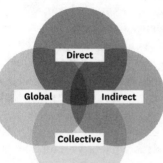

Direct
- Evaluate first-tier suppliers by using sustainability performance indicators that capture their requirements for lower-tier suppliers.
- Survey suppliers on their environmental, health, safety, and labor practices and on their procurement practices.
- Work with major first-tier suppliers to map the firm's supply network.

Indirect
- Provide training and foster peer learning among first-tier suppliers to help them improve their procurement practices with lower-tier suppliers.
- Select high-performing suppliers to pilot new sustainability initiatives.
- Reward suppliers for cascading sustainability requirements to lower-tier suppliers.

Collective
- Commit to developing and complying with industrywide sustainability standards, and help suppliers become full members of industry organizations.
- Via industry organizations, share resources with competitors and major suppliers to achieve sustainability goals.
- Encourage first- and lower-tier suppliers to take advantage of sustainability training programs offered by industry organizations.

Global
- Work closely with relevant NGOs and international institutions interested in improving supply chain sustainability.
- Use tools and data that those organizations provide for dealing with suppliers (contracts and scorecards).
- Recognize suppliers that excel in programs sponsored by NGOs and international institutions.

is effective because the MNCs are hands-on: They offer training to suppliers and provide some incentives for implementing sustainability practices. Most of the first-tier suppliers we interviewed told us that such training had led them to make substantial changes in their manufacturing processes and to begin asking *their* suppliers to adopt similar sustainability standards.

The three MNCs have also created preferred-supplier programs aimed at fostering peer learning about sustainability. One corporation, for instance, invites its most socially and environmentally responsible suppliers to join an exclusive group that enables them to strengthen relationships with the MNC and exchange best sustainability practices with one another. Several of these suppliers have started to set their own sustainability requirements for the suppliers they use.

To further encourage first-tier suppliers to cascade the MNCs' sustainability requirements into their own supply networks, MNCs can use supplier sustainability awards, long-term contracts, and preferred status.

Collective approach

Our MNCs collaborate with their competitors and major suppliers to develop and disseminate industrywide sustainability standards. They recognize that a single MNC cannot be expected to fight alone against the problematic labor or environmental practices of global suppliers. Doing so would be not only prohibitively expensive but also unfair, because in most sectors, the major corporations use many of the same suppliers.

The MNCs we studied are all founding members of industry associations focused on developing sustainability standards, providing assessment tools, and offering training to first- and lower-tier suppliers. One notable association is the Responsible Business Alliance (RBA), whose members include Intel, HP, IBM, Dell, Philips, and Apple.

Collaborative initiatives have many benefits. They can increase efficiencies for suppliers, who can use a standardized self-assessment or audit to satisfy many customers and thus avoid duplication. These initiatives can also draw in more suppliers, because suppliers that have many customers with the same sustainability requirements tend to be more willing to participate. And collaboration can make sustainability initiatives more feasible, because industrywide training is subsidized by members.

Additionally, when MNCs help their first-tier suppliers become full members of an industry association, those suppliers must then comply with industry standards, which means they have to assess their own suppliers' sustainability. The RBA, for example, requires its full members to conduct approved audits annually for at least 25% of their own high-risk facilities *and* 25% of their high-risk suppliers' facilities. (Risk here is assessed along labor, health and safety, environmental, and ethical dimensions.)

Industry associations have a unique power over both first- and lower-tier suppliers, as most of their members are major players in their sectors. Consider the electronics maker Flex, a full member of the RBA and a first-tier supplier for many MNCs. A second-tier electronics supplier is unlikely to refuse a request from Flex for a compliance audit, because it knows that Flex itself has passed this audit and that most other top-tier electronics suppliers, to stay competitive, will probably start issuing similar audit requests.

Global approach

The MNCs we studied make a point of collaborating with international organizations and NGOs that share their goals. For instance, all three corporations have joined the United Nations Global Compact, an international effort to promote corporate social responsibility. The three MNCs also participate in the Carbon Disclosure Project's (CDP's) Supply Chain Program, a global data-collection platform in which suppliers disclose information about their carbon emissions. Firms such as Microsoft, Johnson & Johnson, and Walmart use this platform to engage their suppliers in being transparent about their environmental impact. Several participating suppliers told us that as a result, they are now collecting previously unsolicited information and making investments to try to reduce their carbon footprints.

The progress is encouraging: According to the CDP's 2019 supply chain report, 35% of the program members engaged with their suppliers on climate change in 2018, up from 23% the year before. Additionally, the report noted, "as suppliers become more mature in their understanding of sustainability issues and advance their approaches for taking action, there is evidence that they too are improving in their efforts to cascade positive change downwards through their own supply chains." This is occurring not only because MNCs have asked their suppliers to disclose their carbon emissions but also because that information influences how the MNCs contract with suppliers. One of the corporations we studied has created an award to recognize the suppliers that have improved the most in terms of CDP Supply Chain Program performance. Another MNC includes the program's ratings in its supplier scorecard and monitors those ratings annually.

Room for Improvement

The MNCs in our study have successfully addressed some of the problematic sustainability practices of their suppliers. But as we've already noted, there's plenty of room for improvement in what they're doing. In our research, we identified a few critical shortcomings in their operations when it comes to developing sustainability beyond first-tier suppliers.

First, the MNCs' engineering and procurement units often preapprove lower-tier suppliers, but their vetting criteria don't include social and environmental considerations. In other words, engineering and procurement address only the first of the proverbial three Ps of sustainability (profit), focusing on such issues as cost, quality, delivery, and technology, while overlooking the second and third Ps (people and the planet). Not surprisingly, that can lead to situations in which preapproved lower-tier suppliers violate the sustainability requirements of the MNCs they work with. The first-tier suppliers are then in a tough spot. Like it or not, they have to work with preapproved suppliers—but they are held accountable if those companies mistreat workers or harm the environment. As one exasperated manager said while describing this conundrum, "I am just using the supplier you asked me to use!"

Such predicaments are not uncommon. Different functional units of an MNC (engineering, procurement, sustainability) may pursue different agendas in interacting with first- and lower-tier suppliers—with results that do systemic damage to the corporation's overall sustainability effort and undermine its credibility. To avoid this, MNCs should set convergent sustainability goals and align the incentives for *all* functions that interact with first- and lower-tier suppliers.

A second problem is lack of sustainability training and incentives for procurement officers. All of the 52 procurement employees we interviewed (at MNCs and at suppliers) said they needed more training to properly pursue supplier sustainability on behalf of their firms. Arguably, they need more incentives as well: Companies must reward them for hitting all three Ps—that is, not just cost, quality, and delivery goals but also social and environmental ones. Our research suggests that isn't yet happening in a meaningful way. For the procurement professionals we interviewed, cost savings were unquestionably the top priority, followed by quality improvement and on-time delivery. Social and environmental concerns were notably absent. We should add that although companies at every level of the supply network need to provide more training and incentives for their procurement officers, supplier firms are likely to do so only if MNCs lead the way.

A third shortcoming we observed is that although our three MNCs devote considerable effort to developing their first-tier suppliers' sustainability capabilities, they have little direct contact with their first-tier suppliers' procurement personnel. As a result, those people are poorly informed about the MNCs' sustainability requirements and cannot communicate them clearly to their own suppliers, much less enforce them. To alleviate that problem, MNCs could invite suppliers' procurement personnel to their sustainability training sessions (along with environmental, health, and safety personnel) and encourage them to participate in industrywide sustainability training. Alternatively, MNCs could engage the top executives at their first-tier suppliers and explain the importance of building a sustainable supply network, with the goal of motivating them to catalyze the dissemination of sustainability requirements to lower-tier suppliers.

———————————

Many multinational corporations sincerely want to embed fair labor practices and environmental responsibility throughout their supply networks. A good way to start is by adopting the sustainability strategies used by the three MNCs in our study. But all corporations can and should do more. They should send their suppliers a more consistent message that economic, social, and environmental requirements are *all* important. They should make the same message clear to their procurement officials and create incentives for them to pursue not only economic goals but also environmental and social goals. Those officials should take a hands-on approach to collecting data about suppliers' capacity, monitoring indicators of their sustainability performance, and engaging with them in continuous improvement projects. The MNCs should also work directly with their suppliers' procurement units on the best ways to disseminate sustainability requirements throughout their supply networks. The danger of not acting is clear: A supply chain is only as strong as its weakest link.

Originally published in March–April 2020. Reprint R2002F

How Apple Is Organized for Innovation

by Joel M. Podolny and Morten T. Hansen

APPLE IS WELL KNOWN FOR ITS innovations in hardware, software, and services. Thanks to them, it grew from some 8,000 employees and $7 billion in revenue in 1997, the year Steve Jobs returned, to 137,000 employees and $260 billion in revenue in 2019. Much less well known are the organizational design and the associated leadership model that have played a crucial role in the company's innovation success.

When Jobs arrived back at Apple, it had a conventional structure for a company of its size and scope. It was divided into business units, each with its own P&L responsibilities. General managers ran the Macintosh products group, the information appliances division, and the server products division, among others. As is often the case with decentralized business units, managers were inclined to fight with one another, over transfer prices in particular. Believing that conventional management had stifled innovation, Jobs, in his first year returning as CEO, laid off the general managers of all the business units (in a single day), put the entire company under one P&L, and combined the disparate functional departments of the business units into one functional organization. (See the exhibit "Apple's functional organization.")

Apple's functional organization

In 1997, when Steve Jobs returned to Apple, it had a conventional structure for its size and scope. It was divided into business units, each with its own P&L responsibilities. After retaking the helm, Jobs put the entire company under one P&L and combined the disparate departments of the business units into one functional organization that aligns expertise with decision rights—a structure Apple retains to this day.

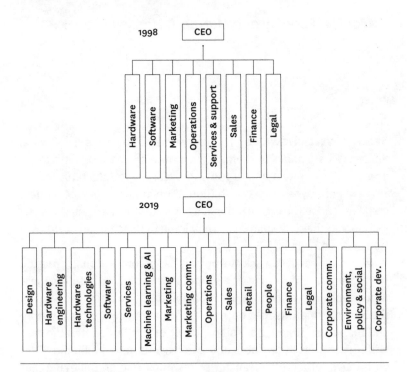

1998

CEO

Hardware · Software · Marketing · Operations · Services & support · Sales · Finance · Legal

2019

CEO

Design · Hardware engineering · Hardware technologies · Software · Services · Machine learning & AI · Marketing · Marketing comm. · Operations · Sales · Retail · People · Finance · Legal · Corporate comm. · Environment, policy & social · Corporate dev.

The adoption of a functional structure may have been unsurprising for a company of Apple's size at the time. What *is* surprising—in fact, remarkable—is that Apple retains it today, even though the company is nearly 40 times as large in terms of revenue and far more complex than it was in 1998. Senior vice presidents are in charge of functions, not products. As was the case with Jobs before him, CEO

Idea in Brief

The Challenge

Major companies competing in many industries struggle to stay abreast of rapidly changing technologies.

One Major Cause

They are typically organized into business units, each with its own set of functions. Thus the key decision makers—the unit leaders—lack a deep understanding of all the domains that answer to them.

The Apple Model

The company is organized around functions, and expertise aligns with decision rights. Leaders are cross-functionally collaborative and deeply knowledgeable about details.

Tim Cook occupies the only position on the organizational chart where the design, engineering, operations, marketing, and retail of any of Apple's main products meet. In effect, besides the CEO, the company operates with no conventional general managers: people who control an entire process from product development through sales and are judged according to a P&L statement.

Business history and organizational theory make the case that as entrepreneurial firms grow large and complex, they must shift from a functional to a multidivisional structure to align accountability and control and prevent the congestion that occurs when countless decisions flow up the org chart to the very top. Giving business unit leaders full control over key functions allows them to do what is best to meet the needs of their individual units' customers and maximize their results, and it enables the executives overseeing them to assess their performance. As the Harvard Business School historian Alfred Chandler documented, U.S. companies such as DuPont and General Motors moved from a functional to a multidivisional structure in the early 20th century. By the latter half of the century the vast majority of large corporations had followed suit. Apple proves that this conventional approach is not necessary and that the functional structure may benefit companies facing tremendous technological change and industry upheaval.

Apple's commitment to a functional organization does not mean that its structure has remained static. As the importance of artificial intelligence and other new areas has increased, that structure has changed. Here we discuss the innovation benefits and leadership challenges of Apple's distinctive and ever-evolving organizational model, which may be useful for individuals and companies wanting to better understand how to succeed in rapidly changing environments.

Why a Functional Organization?

Apple's main purpose is to create products that enrich people's daily lives. That involves not only developing entirely new product categories such as the iPhone and the Apple Watch, but also continually innovating within those categories. Perhaps no product feature better reflects Apple's commitment to continuous innovation than the iPhone camera. When the iPhone was introduced, in 2007, Steve Jobs devoted only six seconds to its camera in the annual keynote event for unveiling new products. Since then iPhone camera technology has contributed to the photography industry with a stream of innovations: High dynamic range imaging (2010), panorama photos (2012), True Tone flash (2013), optical image stabilization (2015), the dual-lens camera (2016), portrait mode (2016), portrait lighting (2017), and night mode (2019) are but a few of the improvements.

To create such innovations, Apple relies on a structure that centers on functional expertise. Its fundamental belief is that those with the most expertise and experience in a domain should have decision rights for that domain. This is based on two views: First, Apple competes in markets where the rates of technological change and disruption are high, so it must rely on the judgment and intuition of people with deep knowledge of the technologies responsible for disruption. Long before it can get market feedback and solid market forecasts, the company must make bets about which technologies and designs are likely to succeed in smartphones, computers, and so on. Relying on technical experts rather than general managers increases the odds that those bets will pay off.

Second, Apple's commitment to offer the best possible products would be undercut if short-term profit and cost targets were the overriding criteria for judging investments and leaders. Significantly, the bonuses of senior R&D executives are based on company-wide performance numbers rather than the costs of or revenue from particular products. Thus product decisions are somewhat insulated from short-term financial pressures. The finance team is not involved in the product road map meetings of engineering teams, and engineering teams are not involved in pricing decisions.

We don't mean to suggest that Apple doesn't consider costs and revenue goals when deciding which technologies and features the company will pursue. It does, but in ways that differ from those employed by conventionally organized companies. Instead of using overall cost and price targets as fixed parameters within which to make design and engineering choices, R&D leaders are expected to weigh the benefits to users of those choices against cost considerations.

In a functional organization, individual and team reputations act as a control mechanism in placing bets. A case in point is the decision to introduce the dual-lens camera with portrait mode in the iPhone 7 Plus in 2016. It was a big wager that the camera's impact on users would be sufficiently great to justify its significant cost.

One executive told us that Paul Hubel, a senior leader who played a central role in the portrait mode effort, was "out over his skis," meaning that he and his team were taking a big risk: If users were unwilling to pay a premium for a phone with a more costly and better camera, the team would most likely have less credibility the next time it proposed an expensive upgrade or feature. The camera turned out to be a defining feature for the iPhone 7 Plus, and its success further enhanced the reputations of Hubel and his team.

It's easier to get the balance right between an attention to costs and the value added to the user experience when the leaders making decisions are those with deep expertise in their areas rather than general managers being held accountable primarily for meeting numerical targets. Whereas the fundamental principle of a conventional business unit structure is to align accountability and control, the fundamental principle of a functional organization is to align expertise and decision rights.

Thus the link between how Apple is organized and the type of innovations it produces is clear. As Chandler famously argued, "structure follows strategy"—even though Apple doesn't use the structure that he anticipated large multinationals would adopt.

Now let's turn to the leadership model underlying Apple's structure.

Three Leadership Characteristics

Ever since Steve Jobs implemented the functional organization, Apple's managers at every level, from senior vice president on down, have been expected to possess three key leadership characteristics: deep expertise that allows them to meaningfully engage in all the work being done within their individual functions; immersion in the details of those functions; and a willingness to collaboratively debate other functions during collective decision-making. When managers have these attributes, decisions are made in a coordinated fashion by the people most qualified to make them.

Deep expertise

Apple is not a company where general managers oversee managers; rather, it is a company where experts lead experts. The assumption is that it's easier to train an expert to manage well than to train a manager to be an expert. At Apple, hardware experts manage hardware, software experts software, and so on. (Deviations from this principle are rare.) This approach cascades down all levels of the organization through areas of ever-increasing specialization. Apple's leaders believe that world-class talent wants to work for and with other world-class talent in a specialty. It's like joining a sports team where you get to learn from and play with the best.

Early on, Steve Jobs came to embrace the idea that managers at Apple should be experts in their area of management. In a 1984 interview he said, "We went through that stage in Apple where we went out and thought, *Oh, we're gonna be a big company, let's hire professional management.* We went out and hired a bunch of professional management. It didn't work at all. . . . They knew how to manage, but they didn't know how to *do* anything. If you're a great person, why do you want to work for somebody you can't learn anything from? And you know what's interesting? You know who the best managers are? They are the great individual contributors who never, ever want to be a manager but decide they have to be . . . because no one else is going to . . . do as good a job."

One current example is Roger Rosner, who heads Apple's software application business, which includes work-productivity apps such as Pages (word processing), Numbers (spreadsheets), and Keynote (presentations) along with GarageBand (music composition), iMovie (movie editing), and News (an app providing news content). Rosner, who studied electrical engineering at Carnegie Mellon, joined Apple in 2001 as a senior engineering manager and rose to become the director of iWork applications, the vice president of productivity apps, and since 2013 the VP of applications. With his deep expertise gained from previous experience as the director of engineering at several smaller software companies, Rosner exemplifies an expert leading experts.

In a functional organization, experts leading experts means that specialists create a deep bench in a given area, where they can learn from one another. For example, Apple's more than 600 experts on camera hardware technology work in a group led by Graham Townsend, a camera expert. Because iPhones, iPads, laptops, and desktop computers all include cameras, these experts would be scattered across product lines if Apple were organized in business units. That would dilute their collective expertise, reducing their power to solve problems and generate and refine innovations.

Immersion in the details

One principle that permeates Apple is "Leaders should know the details of their organization three levels down," because that is essential for speedy and effective cross-functional decision-making at the highest levels. If managers attend a decision-making meeting without the details at their disposal, the decision must either be made without the details or postponed. Managers tell war stories about making presentations to senior leaders who drill down into cells on a spreadsheet, lines of code, or a test result on a product.

Of course, the leaders of many companies insist that they and their teams are steeped in the details. But few organizations match Apple. Consider how its senior leaders pay extreme attention to the exact shape of products' rounded corners. The standard method for rounding corners is to use an arc of a circle to connect the perpendicular sides of a rectangular object, which produces a somewhat abrupt transition from straight to curve. In contrast, Apple's leaders insist on continuous curves, resulting in a shape known in the design community as a "squircle": The slope starts sooner but is less abrupt. (See the exhibit "One example of Apple's attention to detail.") An advantage of hardware products without abrupt changes in curvature is that they produce softer highlights (that is, little to no jump in light reflection along the corner). The difference is subtle, and executing on it isn't simply a matter of a more complicated mathematical formula. It demands that Apple's operations leaders commit to extremely precise manufacturing tolerances to produce millions of

One example of Apple's attention to detail

The standard method for rounding the corners of a rectangular object is to use an arc of a circle to connect the object's perpendicular sides. That can result in an abrupt transition in curvature. To produce softer highlights by minimizing light reflection, Apple uses a "squircle," which creates continuous curves.

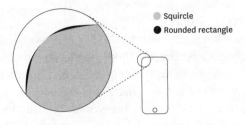

- ○ Squircle
- ● Rounded rectangle

Source: Apple

iPhones and other products with squircles. This deep immersion in detail isn't just a concern that is pushed down to lower-level people; it is central at the leadership level.

Having leaders who are experts in their areas and can go deep into the details has profound implications for how Apple is run. Leaders can push, probe, and "smell" an issue. They know which details are important and where to focus their attention. Many people at Apple see it as liberating, even exhilarating, to work for experts, who provide better guidance and mentoring than a general manager would. Together, all can strive to do the best work of their lives in their chosen area.

Willingness to collaboratively debate

Apple has hundreds of specialist teams across the company, dozens of which may be needed for even one key component of a new product offering. For example, the dual-lens camera with portrait mode required the collaboration of no fewer than 40 specialist teams: silicon design, camera software, reliability engineering, motion sensor hardware, video engineering, core motion, and camera sensor design, to name just a few. How on earth does Apple develop and ship products that require such coordination? The answer is collaborative debate. Because no function is responsible for a product or a service on its own, cross-functional collaboration is crucial.

When debates reach an impasse, as some inevitably do, higher-level managers weigh in as tiebreakers, including at times the CEO and the senior VPs. To do this at speed with sufficient attention to detail is challenging for even the best of leaders, making it all the more important that the company fill many senior positions from within the ranks of its VPs, who have experience in Apple's way of operating.

However, given Apple's size and scope, even the executive team can resolve only a limited number of stalemates. The many horizontal dependencies mean that ineffective peer relationships at the VP and director levels have the potential to undermine not only particular projects but the entire company. Consequently, for people to attain and remain in a leadership position within a function, they must be highly effective collaborators.

That doesn't mean people can't express their points of view. Leaders are expected to hold strong, well-grounded views and advocate forcefully for them, yet also be willing to change their minds when presented with evidence that others' views are better. Doing so is not always easy, of course. A leader's ability to be both partisan and open-minded is facilitated by two things: deep understanding of and devotion to the company's values and common purpose, and a commitment to separating how *right* from how *hard* a particular path is so that the difficulty of executing a decision doesn't prevent its being selected.

The development of the iPhone's portrait mode illustrates a fanatical attention to detail at the leadership level, intense collaborative debate among teams, and the power of a shared purpose to shape and ultimately resolve debates. In 2009 Hubel had the idea of developing an iPhone feature that would allow people to take portrait photos with *bokeh*—a Japanese term that refers to the pleasing blurring of a background—which photography experts generally consider to be of the highest quality. At that time only expensive single-lens reflex cameras could take such photos, but Hubel thought that with a dual-lens design and advanced computational-photography techniques, Apple could add the capability in the iPhone. His idea aligned well with the camera team's stated purpose: "More people taking better images more of the time."

As the team worked to turn this idea into reality, several challenges emerged. The first attempts produced some amazing portrait pictures but also a number of "failure cases" in which the algorithm was unable to distinguish between the central object in sharp relief (a face, for instance) and the background being blurred. For example, if a person's face was to be photographed from behind chicken wire, it was not possible to construct an algorithm that would capture the chicken wire to the side of the face with the same sharpness as the chicken wire in front of it. The wire to the side would be as blurred as the background.

One might say, "Who cares about the chicken wire case? That's exceedingly rare." But for the team, sidestepping rare or extreme situations—what engineers call *corner cases*—would violate Apple's strict engineering standard of zero "artifacts," meaning "any unde-sired or unintended alteration in data introduced in a digital process by an involved technique and/or technology." Corner cases sparked "many tough discussions" between the camera team and other teams involved, recalls Myra Haggerty, the VP of sensor software and UX prototyping, who oversaw the firmware and algorithm teams. Sebastien Marineau-Mes, the VP to whom the camera software team ultimately reported, decided to defer the release of the feature until the following year to give the team time to better address failure cases—"a hard pill to swallow," Hubel admits.

To get some agreement on quality standards, the engineering teams invited senior design and marketing leaders to meet, figur-ing that they would offer a new perspective. The design leaders brought an additional artistic sensibility to the debate, asking, "What makes a beautiful portrait?" To help reassess the zero-artifacts standard, they collected images from great portrait pho-tographers. They noted, among other things, that these photos often had blurring at the edges of a face but sharpness on the eyes. So they charged the algorithm teams with achieving the same effect. When the teams succeeded, they knew they had an accept-able standard.

Another issue that emerged was the ability to preview a portrait photo with a blurred background. The camera team had designed the feature so that users could see its effect on their photos only *after* they had been taken, but the human interface (HI) design team pushed back, insisting that users should be able to see a "live pre-view" and get some guidance about how to make adjustments *before* taking the photo. Johnnie Manzari, a member of the HI team, gave the camera team a demo. "When we saw the demo, we realized that this is what we needed to do," Townsend told us. The members of his camera hardware team weren't sure they could do it, but diffi-culty was not an acceptable excuse for failing to deliver what would clearly be a superior user experience. After months of engineering effort, a key stakeholder, the video engineering team (responsible for the low-level software that controls sensor and camera opera-tions) found a way, and the collaboration paid off. Portrait mode was central to Apple's marketing of the iPhone 7 Plus. It proved a major reason for users' choosing to buy and delighting in the use of the phone.

As this example shows, Apple's collaborative debate involves people from various functions who disagree, push back, promote or reject ideas, and build on one another's ideas to come up with the best solutions. It requires open-mindedness from senior leaders. It also requires those leaders to inspire, prod, or influence colleagues in other areas to contribute toward achieving their goals.

While Townsend is accountable for how great the camera is, he needed dozens of other teams—each of which had a long list of its own commitments—to contribute their time and effort to the portrait mode project. At Apple that's known as *accountability without control:* You're accountable for making the project succeed even though you don't control all the other teams. This process can be messy yet produce great results. "Good mess" happens when various teams work with a shared purpose, as in the case of the portrait mode project. "Bad mess" occurs when teams push their own agendas ahead of common goals. Those who become associated with bad mess and don't or can't change their behavior are removed from leadership positions, if not from Apple altogether.

Leadership at Scale

Apple's way of organizing has led to tremendous innovation and success over the past two decades. Yet it has not been without challenges, especially with revenues and head count having exploded since 2008.

As the company has grown, entering new markets and moving into new technologies, its functional structure and leadership model have had to evolve. Deciding how to organize areas of expertise to best enable collaboration and rapid decision-making has been an important responsibility of the CEO. The adjustments Tim Cook has implemented in recent years include dividing the hardware function into hardware engineering and hardware technologies; adding artificial intelligence and machine learning as a functional area; and moving human interface out of software to merge it with industrial design, creating an integrated design function.

Another challenge posed by organizational growth is the pressure it imposes on the several hundred VPs and directors below the executive team. If Apple were to cap the size or scope of a senior leader's organization to limit the number and breadth of details that the leader is expected to own, the company would need to hugely expand the number of senior leaders, making the kind of collaboration that has worked so well impossible to preserve.

Cognizant of this problem, Apple has been quite disciplined about limiting the number of senior positions to minimize how many leaders must be involved in any cross-functional activity. In 2006, the year before the iPhone's launch, the company had some 17,000 employees; by 2019 that number had grown more than eightfold, to 137,000. Meanwhile, the number of VPs approximately doubled, from 50 to 96. The inevitable result is that senior leaders head larger and more diverse teams of experts, meaning more details to oversee and new areas of responsibility that fall outside their core expertise.

In response, many Apple managers over the past five years or so have been evolving the leadership approach described above: experts leading experts, immersion in the details, and collaborative debate. We have codified these adaptions in what we call the *discretionary leadership* model, which we have incorporated into a new educational program for Apple's VPs and directors. Its purpose is to address the challenge of getting this leadership approach to drive innovation in all areas of the company, not just product development, at an ever-greater scale.

When Apple was smaller, it may have been reasonable to expect leaders to be experts on and immersed in the details of pretty much everything going on in their organizations. However, they now need to exercise greater discretion regarding where and how they spend their time and efforts. They must decide which activities demand their full attention to detail because those activities create the most value for Apple. Some of those will fall within their existing core expertise (what they still need to *own*), and some will require them to *learn* new areas of expertise. Activities that require less attention from the leader can be pushed down to others (and the leaders will either *teach* others or *delegate* in cases where they aren't experts).

Rosner, the VP of applications, provides a good example. Like many other Apple managers, he has had to contend with three challenges arising from Apple's tremendous growth. First, the *size* of his function has exploded over the past decade in terms of both head count (from 150 to about 1,000) and the number of projects under way at any given time. Clearly, he cannot dive into all the details of all those projects. Second, the *scope* of his portfolio has widened: Over the past 10 years he has assumed responsibility for new applications, including News, Clips (video editing), Books, and Final Cut Pro (advanced video editing). Although apps are his core area of expertise, some aspects of these—among them editorial content for News, how book publishing works, and video editing—involve matters in which Rosner is not an expert. Finally, as Apple's product portfolio and number of projects have expanded, even more coordination with other functions is required, increasing the *complexity* of collaborating across the many units. For instance, whereas Rosner is responsible for the engineering side of News, other managers oversee the operating system on which it depends, the content, and the business relationships with content creators (such as the *New York Times*) and advertisers.

To cope, Rosner has adapted his role. As an expert who leads other experts, he had been immersed in details—especially those concerning the top-level aspects of software applications and their architecture that affect how users engage with the software. He also collaborated with managers across the company in projects that involved those areas.

But with the expansion of his responsibilities, he has moved some things from his *owning* box—including traditional productivity apps such as Keynote and Pages—into his *teaching* box. (See the exhibit "Roger Rosner's discretionary leadership.") Now he guides and gives feedback to other team members so that they can develop software applications according to Apple's norms. Being a teacher doesn't mean that Rosner gives instruction at a whiteboard; rather, he offers strong, often passionate critiques of his team's work. (Clearly, gen-

Roger Rosner's discretionary leadership

Apple's VP of applications, Roger Rosner, oversees a portfolio comprising four distinct categories that require varying amounts of his time and attention to detail. In 2019 it looked like this:

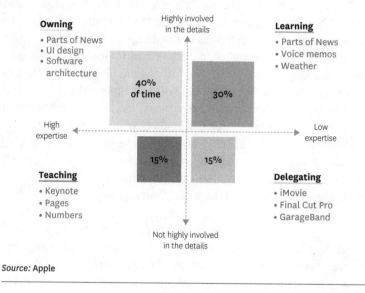

Owning
- Parts of News
- UI design
- Software architecture

Highly involved in the details

Learning
- Parts of News
- Voice memos
- Weather

40% of time

30%

High expertise

Low expertise

15%

15%

Teaching
- Keynote
- Pages
- Numbers

Delegating
- iMovie
- Final Cut Pro
- GarageBand

Not highly involved in the details

Source: Apple

eral managers without his core expertise would find it difficult to teach what they don't know.)

The second challenge for Rosner involved the addition of activities beyond his original expertise. Six years ago he was given responsibility for the engineering and design of News. Consequently, he had to learn about publishing news content via an app—to understand news publications, digital advertising, machine learning to personalize news content, architecting for privacy, and how to incentivize publishers. Thus some of his work fell into the *learning* box. Here managers face a steep learning curve to acquire new skills. Given how demanding this is, only critical new activities should fall into this category. Over six years of intense learning, Rosner has mastered some of these areas, which are now in his owning box.

As long as a particular activity remains in the learning box, leaders must adopt a beginner's mindset, questioning subordinates in a way that suggests they don't already know the answer (because they don't). This differs starkly from the way leaders question subordinates about activities in the owning and teaching boxes.

Finally, Rosner has delegated some areas—including iMovie and GarageBand, in which he is not an expert—to people with the requisite capabilities. For activities in the *delegating* box, he assembles teams, agrees on objectives, monitors and reviews progress, and holds the teams accountable: the stuff of general management.

Whereas Apple's VPs spend most of their time in the owning and learning boxes, general managers at other companies tend to spend most of their time in the delegating box. Rosner estimates that he spends about 40% of his time on activities he owns (including collaboration with others in a given area), about 30% on learning, about 15% on teaching, and about 15% on delegating. These numbers vary by manager, of course, depending on their business and the needs at a given time.

The discretionary leadership model preserves the fundamental principle of an effective functional organization at scale—aligning expertise and decision rights. Apple can effectively move into new areas when leaders like Rosner take on new responsibilities outside their original expertise, and teams can grow in size when leaders teach others their craft and delegate work. We believe that Apple will continue to innovate and prosper by being organized this way.

Apple's functional organization is rare, if not unique, among very large companies. It flies in the face of prevailing management theory that companies should be reorganized into divisions and business units as they become large. But something vital gets lost in a shift to business units: the alignment of decision rights with expertise.

Why do companies so often cling to having general managers in charge of business units? One reason, we believe, is that making the change is difficult. It entails overcoming inertia, reallocating power among managers, changing an individual-oriented incentive system, and learning new ways of collaborating. That is daunting when a company already faces huge external challenges. An intermediate step may be to cultivate the experts-leading-experts model even within a business unit structure. For example, when filling the next senior management role, pick someone with deep expertise in that area as opposed to someone who might make the best general manager. But a full-fledged transformation requires that leaders also transition to a functional organization. Apple's track record proves that the rewards may justify the risks. Its approach can produce extraordinary results.

Originally published in November–December 2020. Reprint R2006F

MORRA AARONS-MELE is the founder of the award-winning social impact agency, Women Online, and author of *Hiding in the Bathroom.* She has written for the *New York Times,* the *Wall Street Journal, O the Oprah Magazine,* and other publications, and is the host of *The Anxious Achiever* podcast.

BORIS BABIC is an assistant professor of decision sciences at INSEAD.

HANNAH RILEY BOWLES is the Roy E. Larsen Senior Lecturer in Public Policy and Management at Harvard Kennedy School.

ADAM BRANDENBURGER is the J. P. Valles Professor at the Stern School of Business, a distinguished professor at the Tandon School of Engineering, and the faculty director of the Program on Creativity and Innovation at NYU Shanghai, all at New York University.

TOMAS CHAMORRO-PREMUZIC is the Chief Talent Scientist at ManpowerGroup, a professor of business psychology at University College London and at Columbia University, and an associate at Harvard's Entrepreneurial Finance Lab. He is the author of *Why Do So Many Incompetent Men Become Leaders? (and How to Fix It),* upon which his TEDx talk was based. Find him on Twitter: @drtcp.

PRITHWIRAJ (RAJ) CHOUDHURY is the Lumry Family Associate Professor of Business Administration at Harvard Business School. His research focuses on the future of work—especially how work-from-anywhere practices are changing its geography.

I. GLENN COHEN is a deputy dean, professor of law, and faculty director of the Petrie-Flom Center for Health Law Policy, Biotechnology, and Bioethics at Harvard Law School.

ROBIN J. ELY is the Diane Doerge Wilson Professor of Business Administration at Harvard Business School and the faculty chair of the HBS Gender Initiative.

THEODOROS EVGENIOU is a professor of decision sciences and technology management at INSEAD.

FRANCES FREI is the UPS Foundation Professor of Service Management at Harvard Business School. She received shares in Uber as compensation for her work with the company, which she continues to hold. She is one of the authors of *Unleashed: The Unapologetic Leader's Guide to Empowering Everyone Around You* (Harvard Business Review Press, 2020).

GRETCHEN GAVETT is a senior editor at *Harvard Business Review.*

SARA GERKE is a research fellow in medicine, artificial intelligence, and law at the Petrie-Flom Center.

DENNIS A. GIOIA is the Robert and Judith Auritt Klein Professor of Management at the Smeal College of Business at Penn State University.

MORTEN T. HANSEN is a member of Apple University's faculty and a professor at the University of California, Berkeley. He was formerly on the faculties of Harvard Business School and INSEAD.

DOUGLAS HOLT is the founder and president of the Cultural Strategy Group and was formerly a professor at Harvard Business School and the University of Oxford. He is the author of *How Brands Become Icons: The Principles of Cultural Branding* (Harvard Business School Press, 2004).

ROBERT LIVINGSTON is the author of *The Conversation: How Seeking and Speaking the Truth About Racism Can Radically Transform Individuals and Organizations.* He also serves on the faculty of the Harvard Kennedy School.

ANNE MORRISS is an entrepreneur and the executive founder of the Leadership Consortium. She is one of the authors of *Unleashed: The*

Unapologetic Leader's Guide to Empowering Everyone Around You (Harvard Business Review Press, 2020).

BARRY NALEBUFF is the Milton Steinbach Professor of Management at the Yale School of Management, where he teaches negotiation, innovation, strategy, and game theory.

JOEL M. PODOLNY is a vice president of Apple and the dean of Apple University. Prior to joining Apple, in 2009, he was the dean of the Yale School of Management and on the faculty of Harvard's and Stanford's business schools.

DAVID A. THOMAS is the president of Morehouse College. He is also the H. Naylor Fitzhugh Professor Emeritus at Harvard Business School and the former dean of Georgetown University's McDonough School of Business.

BOBBI THOMASON is an assistant professor of applied behavioral science at Pepperdine University.

VERÓNICA H. VILLENA is an assistant professor of supply chain management at the Smeal College of Business at Penn State University.

Index

Engage with HBR content the way you want, on any device.

With HBR's new subscription plans, you can access world-renowned **case studies** from Harvard Business School and receive **four free eBooks**. Download and customize prebuilt **slide decks and graphics** from our **Visual Library**. With HBR's archive, top 50 best-selling articles, and five new articles every day, HBR is more than just a magazine.

Subscribe Today
hbr.org/success

The most important management ideas all in one place.

We hope you enjoyed this book from *Harvard Business Review*. Now you can get even more with HBR's 10 Must Reads Boxed Set. From books on leadership and strategy to managing yourself and others, this 6-book collection delivers articles on the most essential business topics to help you succeed.

HBR's 10 Must Reads Series

The definitive collection of ideas and best practices on our most sought-after topics from the best minds in business.

- Change Management
- Collaboration
- Communication
- Emotional Intelligence
- Innovation
- Leadership
- Making Smart Decisions

- Managing Across Cultures
- Managing People
- Managing Yourself
- Strategic Marketing
- Strategy
- Teams
- The Essentials

hbr.org/mustreads

Buy for your team, clients, or event.
Visit hbr.org/bulksales for quantity discount rates.